NEGOTIATION

Process, Tactics, Theory

Second Edition

David Churchman

University Press of America, Inc.
Lanham • New York • London

Copyright © 1995 by
University Press of America,® Inc.
4720 Boston Way
Lanham, Maryland 20706

3 Henrietta Street
London, WC2E 8LU England

Library of Congress Cataloging-in-Publication Data

Churchman, David
Negotiation : process, tactics, theory / David Churchman.--2nd ed.
p. cm.
Includes bibliographical references.
1. Negotiation. 2. Conflict management. 3. Negotiation in business.
I. Churchman, David. Negotiation tactics. II. Title.
BF637.N4C48   1995   302.3--dc20   95-10748 CIP

ISBN 0-8191-9946-X (cloth: alk: paper)
ISBN 0-8191-9947-8 (pbk: alk: paper)

Contents

Alternate Names:

Figures

The Negotiation Process

Negotiation is a tool. Just as a hammer is useful for driving nails but not for cutting wood, negotiation is useful for resolving some but not all disputes. It is useless if parties have nothing in common to motivate settling their differences. It is unlikely to settle differences in belief, as the history of theological disputes testifies. It is even less likely to change Man's nature, however much idealists see negotiation as a panacea for conflict.

Fortunately, a communist and a capitalist do not have to resolve differences of belief concerning the morality of profit to complete a sale. Plea bargaining can succeed even if prosecution and defense differ on the causes of crime. The Soviet Union and the United States did not have to settle which was the imperialist to reduce the number of missiles and troops in Europe. Iran and the United States did not have to end their general antagonism before the embassy hostages could be freed.

Negotiation becomes possible when common needs motivate parties to settle specific differences. Plea bargaining deprives victims of maximum revenge, and district attorneys of maximum political gain, but saves the cost of a trial and insures conviction. From the viewpoint of the accused, plea bargaining removes the risk of a long sentence but gives up any chance of acquittal. Men and women who abhor one another find ways to preserve the appearance of their marriages for the sake of their careers or their children. During the U.S. Constitutional Convention, large states wanted legislative representation based on population; small ones wanted equal representation for each state. But, ineffective government under the Articles of Confederation and the shared experience of the Revolution provided common interests that led to creation of a bicameral legislature balancing the interests of both large and small states.

Complexity is independent of importance. An important negotiation may involve no more than simple haggling over a single issue, such as the number of righteous men needed to save Sodom from God's wrath (Genesis XVIII). Buying a rug in Istanbul's Covered Bazaar, less important but more complex, involves issues such as currency, price, shipping, and insurance. Labor contracts, home purchases, corporate mergers, environmental disputes, and peace negotiations involve dozens of issues. Uncertainties such as inflation, exchange rates, untried technologies, regulatory costs, the likelihood of litigation, or the stability of a government complicate many negotiations.

Taking all these points into consideration, and borrowing from Ikle (1964), negotiation is a process in which proposals are put forward for the ostensible purpose of resolving specific disagreements among two or more parties with both conflicting and common interests. Each word is meaningful. For example, at the turn of the century the British consul Milner wanted his negotiations with Boer President Kruger to fail. Despite his government's wish for accommodation, Milner wanted war so his country could take over *all* of what became South Africa. His proposals were only "ostensibly" for the purpose of resolving differences (Pakenham, 1979).

Two very distinct negotiating strategies are said to exist. Integrative, or win-win, bargaining is very much the rage. Whether or not win-win is superior, most negotiations are distributive or win-lose. Learning only one strategy is like coaching a football team in offense but not defense: disastrous! This book provides tactics for win-lose negotiations, and argues that the difference, measured by results obtained, is much exaggerated.

Tactics provide the means by which negotiators pursue their goals. Football again provides a useful analogy. The goal is to outscore the other team. The tactics by which the goal is pursued include a dazzling variety of passes such as the bomb, button hook, flare, fly, play action, post, roll out, screen, slant in, square in, and square out. In football as in negotiation, every tactic works some of the time; no tactic works every time. Success depends on skillful execution, good timing and luck--which in that overused phrase, a team makes for itself. The best team wins most of the time, but upsets do occur.

Unlike football, there is nothing arcane about negotiating tactics. The revelation will not be the tactics, but their familiarity and how early in life you began to use them. Familiarity should not be confused with mastery. There is a difference in the way a high school and a professional football team execute plays. There is a similar difference in the way novices and experts use negotiation tactics.

Negotiation is like football in other ways as well. Most important, both take time and move through phases. Every writer divides the negotiation process differently. Academics alone get exercised about such matters. Everyone else realizes the disputes are about as productive as trying to establish one temperature at which water becomes "cold" for all purposes. One useful formulation divides negotiation into Preparation, Exploration, Bargaining, and Closing phases. The first phase, the least tactical of the four, is discussed below in more detail than the remaining three.

Preparation

Preparation includes identifying issues, defining one's own needs, and learning as much as possible about those of opponents. It might include role playing, using computer models to aid decision making, and negotiation team formation. These considerations are closely interrelated. Teams must work together and with opponents so intra- and inter-personal relations must be considered. The last-minute negotiations to oust General Cedras from Haiti provide a good example of this aspect of team formation. President Carter knew Cedras but he has proven himself naive, feckless, over-sympathetic to dictators. Senator Nunn was included to keep the former president under control, and General Powell was included so General Cedras could surrender to an equal.

Teams have four or five major roles. They may have more roles than people, requiring several tasks of some individuals. They may have more people than roles, with some roles subdivided among specialists. Teams may have supernumeraries whose sole task is to make their team larger and more imposing than the opponents'.

The first role is chief negotiator. The chief negotiator usually does most of the talking, controls when and what other team members say, and has the greatest decision-making authority. These functions can be divided and in some cultures commonly are. Speakers may be relatively junior individuals chosen for their language skills. There may be spokesmen for specialities such as financial, legal, or technical matters.

The second role is file management. On the surface the task is simple: find the papers with the information requested. Team effectiveness is enhanced by a file manager who anticipates needs and knows when to pretend the information is not available.

The third role on a negotiating team is the observer. In some teams, this role is assigned to the senior team member. This is considered clever by those who do so, and devious by those to whom it is done. Observers assess opponents and watch for opportunities to divide them against one another. They estimate objectives, deadlines, minimum acceptable agreements. They listen for signals that speakers may be too involved to notice. Sometimes a second observer is assigned to watch one's own team for inadvertent signals!

The fourth role is recorder. Record all agreements, no matter how minor, but all offers too. Memory is unreliable, people change. The team that controls the record often gains small advantages. This makes it worth volunteering for the responsibility of keeping the minutes of a negotiation. If that is impossible, seek joint responsibility. If that is thwarted, keep an independent record to check against the official one. In multilingual situations, additional care is vital. Try to have your language as the official one and provide translators for opponents. If that is impossible, make sure both languages are official. Never depend on translators provided by opponents.

The fifth role (if relevant) is press representative. Once negotiators take a public stand, it is hard to change positions. "I never saw anything good come of public disclosure and discussion of negotiating positions (Brooks, Spring 1994). Try to limit announcements to agreements already reached. Every team member should refer *all* questions to the press representative. The press representative should answer or evade questions according to plan. Any other team member quoted in the press or identified as the source of an unauthorized comment should be fired and disavowed. It is not unheard of to stage leaks, disavowals, and firings to mislead or signal opponents or to persuade constituents that everything possible is being done.

Exploration

The Exploration Phase involves explaining your needs to the opponents, learning theirs, and establishing the bargaining climate (discussed below). Use this phase both to communicate your needs to opponents and to improve your understanding of how the situation looks to them. This is not the same as being sympathetic to their point of view. Negotiations are adversarial; negotiators seek to advance their interests.

One danger during this phase is revealing too much without getting comparable information from opponents in return. Negotiators quickly learn that "laying all your cards on the table" without seeing all of the opponents' is dangerous. It leaves opponents able to meet your minimum needs while continually demanding more from you to meet their needs. Therefore, especially during the Exploration Phase, it generally is best to listen as much as you talk.

Bargaining

The Bargaining Phase consists primarily of offering and discussing specific proposals. Negotiators often begin by indicating opponent's remarks were understood, give hope of eventual settlement, but contain elements that remain unacceptable. Their proposals frequently begin or end with explanations and justifications (see the discussion of acceptance time in the next section). Proposals always include an offer, sometimes conditions or time limits. They can close with a request for a response intended to prevent the opponent feeling settlement is impossible and to keep the process going. To the extent concessions are made, each iteration reduces the distance among opponents, bringing settlement closer.

Closing

The Closing Phase becomes possible when the current proposal meets the needs of each party. Signals may indicate the time to move into this phase. The major elements are agreeing to terms and ratification. Closing tactics play the major part in reaching agreement, and are discussed in the next section. Ratification is common when agents carry out negotiations for principals ranging from nations to sports figures and varies considerably in how it is conducted. Negotiators sometimes have as much difficulty obtaining ratification as they have in coming to terms with opponents.

The closing phase may also include provision for settling disagreements over interpretation and provide for their resolution. It may include provison for contingencies, monitoring devices, performance bonds, and penalty clauses.

Conclusion

Actual negotiations seldom follow such rigid patterns. Real negotiations move back and forth among the phases. Negotiators may caucus to revise goals, or resume bargaining when resistance proves they tried to close too soon. Some negotiations are characterized by interruptions. Some negotiations might go through the four phases issue-by-issue. Others might go through each issue phase-by-phase. Some will prove a messy mix of both approaches. Multi-party negotiations are even less predictable.

Each phase requires negotiation tactics, the main subject of this book. Most can be used in all four phases. To take an extreme example, closing tactics may be necessary in the preparation phase if a negotiating team is ever to reach agreement on its own goals.

None of the tactics in this book are original, and none can be attributed to a single author. Children learn some of them by the time they are three, as any parent can testify. For example, there is the eight year old who got the tacos she wanted by saying "What if I practice my violin every day." Called a day later for not practicing, she replied, "I said 'What if?'" There was much talk in the 1980s about negotiation as an innovation to reduce the financial and psychic costs of divorce. But, Romer (1984) describes a divorce negotiation conducted in Egypt about 1200 BC.

Diplomats negotiating nuclear arms limitation treaties would recognize the tactics of Sumerian merchants trading copper and lapis lazuli four thousand years ago. Teenagers wishing to stay out late would recognize the tactics of labor negotiators seeking higher wages for their members. Plea bargaining lawyers are reminiscent of medieval Polish parents negotiating a dowry. Manufacturers negotiate with wholesalers, wholesalers with retailers, retailers with consumers. Unions negotiate salary and benefits for their members. Executives negotiate salary and "perks" such as corner offices, company cars, and first class air travel. Whatever the place, whatever the time, whatever the subject, negotiators have tried to reach agreement using the same basic tactics.

Tactics that have been found so useful for so long under so many circumstances do not depend on mere trickery or the stupidity of opponents. It is wiser to think of them as ways by which negotiators explore the possible existence of, and move toward, a mutually beneficial settlement that all can accept.

Despite the universality of negotiating tactics, there is no agreement on what they are called or how many there are. For example, "linkage," "log rolling," "packaging" or "tie-ins," could be treated as four tactics, or as variations of one. Combining them risks obscuring subtle differences. Discussing them separately risks repetition and proliferation. I take the first risk in hope of providing a shorter, less pedantic, and more useful book.

Despite the arbitrary nature of the names for each tactic, they are discussed in alphabetical order. Some say there must be a more useful arrangement--but have not suggested one that works. The main reason is that each tactic can be used at any time in combination with, or in opposition to, almost any other tactic or combination of tactics.

Negotiation Tactics

Acceptance Time

Negotiators often begin with unrealistic settlement goals. One function of negotiation is to give all parties time to adjust to realistic ideas of what can be achieved. This requires "acceptance" time.

Early in negotiations, acceptance time is used to convince opponents they must reduce their aspirations if they want an agreement. Bluntness is counterproductive so offers often follow long explanations. This implies that the offer is serious, whether it is or not. Alternatively, negotiators may be apologetic, servile, wheedling, or may ask for mercy or sympathy. Whatever the words, their tone and length are intended to soften the impact of a disappointing offer. Skillfully done, opponents will even feel relief that the offer is better than they expected!

Late in the bargaining phase, offers should precede explanations, reversing the early order. The idea is to convince opponents (rightly or wrongly) that no more concessions will be made, and to prevent them rejecting proposals without thinking.

During the closing phase, acceptance time helps opponents adjust psychologically. Therefore, explanation and proposal are abbreviated, but the request for a fair and considered reply can be extensive.

Agenda

Agendas can be written or explicit, which is common in union contracts, government procurements, or international treaties. They can be unwritten or implicit, which is common in sales negotiations, family disputes, plea bargaining, and legislative conferences. In the latter case, people often become frustrated with an apparent lack of progress, forget concessions, or raise new issues at the last moment. Frequent summaries are useful.

Negotiators can seek advantage by controlling the completeness, order, or phrasing of the agenda. An example of an incomplete agenda is a car salesman's omission of taxes, license and preparation fees during negotiation. Negotiators protect themselves by identifying all issues in advance. They can then make sure all issues are addressed, or can adjust their proposals to allow for a surprise at the end.

Advantage can be sought from the order in which items are discussed. A buyer may be most concerned with delivery date, down, and monthly payments; the seller with interest income, risk of default, and eliminating slower selling items from inventory. Other aspects of the sale, such as options and warranties may vary in importance among parties. Two factors must be considered in seeking an advantage from the order in which items appear on the agenda.

The first factor is whether to address an issue early or late. Simply because energy declines with time, issues discussed late tend to be resolved more quickly and less carefully. A salesman might try to negotiate high-profit items last. A buyer can exploit a salesman's fear of losing a sale after putting in a lot of effort by addressing important things late, and suddenly getting tough. Negotiators under deadline pressure usually prefer to deal with major issues first. Those in weak positions may prefer to deal with them last.

The second factor in ordering the agenda is how much can be conceded on each issue.   A negotiator may want unimportant issues settled first so large concessions can be made and compensation requested later in the interest of "fairness." This is most likely to work if opponents are naive, or if the parties have a long-term relationship. It may backfire if opponents interpret early concessions as a sign of weakness. It may work to all parties advantage if issues are not equally important to each, a concept so important that it is discussed separately (see Linkage).

Another approach is to phrase agenda items to one's own advantage. The goal is to place the opponents on the defensive from the start. A classic example of this is the agenda that was proposed by the Communist side for the Korean War truce talks. For example, the phrasing of the first item was:

> Establishment of the 38th parallel as the military demarcation line between both sides, and establishment of a demilitarized zone, as basic consideration for the cessation of hostilities in Korea (Joy, 1970).

The 38th parallel had been the prewar boundary between North and South Korea. At the time of the truce talks the North Koreans possessed a small area south of the parallel, the United Nations a much larger area north of it. The phrasing was an attempt to embed UN concessions in the agenda. It is legitimate to seek advantage from the agenda. If all parties do so, a fair agenda usually results. The UN negotiators resisted. It took ten sessions to achieve neutral phrasing. The first item finally read:

> Fixing a military demarcation line between both sides so as to establish a demilitarized zone as a basic condition for the cessation of hostilities in Korea (Joy, 1970).

Ambiguity

Teachers encourage clarity and precision in speaking and writing. Judges require us to tell the truth, the whole truth, and nothing but the truth. Our litigiousness requires trying to anticipate and provide for every eventuality in our contracts. When clarity and precision protect negotiators, they make agreement easier.

However, clarity can make agreement harder by focusing attention on what can go wrong. Spelling out every detail can overemphasize minor matters, and exacerbate or even create differences. Expressing sympathy for opponents' needs without making substantive concessions can improve the bargaining climate. Ambiguous statements can keep talks going simply because they require clarification. Ambiguous demands make face-saving concessions easier. Having to clarify an imprecise statement usually is better than having to equivocate after making a precise one.

Ambiguity can make it possible to reach agreement, to postpone issues or to prevent a difficult one standing in the way of an otherwise useful agreement. The technique is not new. Around 1280 BC Egyptians and Hittites negotiated a treaty that allowed each side to assert that it was the other who had sued for peace (Wilson, 1951). In 1993 and again in 1994 Cedras of Haiti refused to "quit" but agreed to "retire early." The change of phrase allowed both sides to portray the agreement in a favorable light to their own constituents. Ambiguity does not create problems if all parties are clear on what they must, can, and cannot do.

Ambiguous statements or definitions also can provide the time and flexibility needed to implement agreements. Syria has long demanded Israeli withdrawal *from* the Golan Heights, while Israel will only promise to withdraw *on* the Golan Heights--a significant difference. This might be resolved by a phrase such as "Israel makes no claim of sovereignty to the Golan Heights." Such a statement implies Israeli withdrawal, but does not specify when or how. It allows for phased withdrawals over time as and if trust develops between the two sides. An automobile body shop owner regarded her plant-filled raspberry-painted 1975 Mustang as a work of art. City inspectors said it was a junk car and had to be removed. Reclassifying it as a sign for which there was a $25 fee left everyone satisfied. Reversing her strategy, when the owner of a rhythm and blues club in a nearby city was told his 62 foot tall blue saxophone violated the height limit on signs, having it declared a work of art saved his saxophone (*WSJ*, 11 August 1994).

Negotiators can use a thesaurus to find the words with just the right tone. Numbers can be approximate or precise. Approximations can be high or low. Probabilities--particularly joint probabilities with incomplete information--are difficult to interpret. Should you carry your umbrella if there is a 60% chance of rain and a 35% chance that you will lose it. How long you will you be outdoors, how heavy will the rain be, and how expensive is the umbrella? Facts and assumptions can be merged, particularly when they involve such matters as currency exchanges, depreciation, future value, indirect costs, inflation, risk, or return on investment must be considered. The return on a flat-rate mortgage is precise unless it can be paid off early. Licensing agreements can be based on a flat fee or a percentage of sales.

Decimals make things look more precise and can be created by almost any calculation requiring division. "Average" is the mean to most people, but medians and modes also are averages (only in symmetrical curves are they identical). In skewed curves, such as income or life expectancy, the mean always is nearer the tail than the mode, with the median between. Negotiators should calculate all three and choose the most advantageous. Both the calculation and appropriateness of opponents' averages should be questioned. For example, if offered the "average" starting salary for a position, point out that you are being hired because you are better than average.

Anger

Anger is common in negotiations. We get angry with opponents. They get angry with us. We may try to make opponents angry, but must insure they do not do so to us. Screaming and banging things about are the normal form, but quiet rage may be more effective. Anger can be real or feigned. Figure 1 clarifies the possibilities.

You might fake anger to show opponents that an issue is important to you or that you are about to deadlock. You can fake it to convince opponents that they have pushed you as far as possible (true or not). You can fake anger if you are being treated unfairly, or to try to shame opponents into concessions.

If your anger is real, your judgment suffers, talks may break down, opportunities for settlement may be missed, you may concede too much. Negotiators should train themselves never to lose their temper, and to request a break when they fail to achieve this difficult ideal.

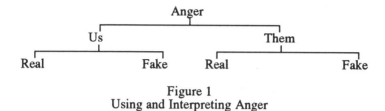

Figure 1
Using and Interpreting Anger

Some say the shoe Nikita Khrushchev banged on the table at the United Nations was an extra carried in his brief case. The more experienced your opponents are, the more likely they are faking anger for some purpose. Real anger often is preceded, but false anger followed, by nonverbal clues such as flashing eyes and a reddening face.

Opponents who really get angry (or cry, or otherwise lose control) are likely to make errors: make sure they are in your favor. Once they calm down, they sometimes can be shamed into concessions.

An opponent's anger is a dangerous opportunity. False anger interpreted as real may win concessions from you, or cause you to miss the signal intended. Real anger interpreted as a ploy, or leading you to anger in response, can undermine the bargaining climate or even end the talks. It takes considerable experience to remain cool in the face of anger. If in doubt, take a break until things calm down. Or, you can hear your opponents out, decide if their anger is real or feigned, and choose your approach accordingly. Real or fake, never allow anger to intimidate you into making concessions.

Finally, instead of merely waiting for an opponent to get angry, you can try to make them lose their temper. Bad faith negotiation might work (and may be the reason opponents are practicing it on you). Showing up late, forgetting documents, exhaustive exploration of grammatical points, revisiting settled points, discourtesy, feigned stupidity, spilling coffee, rejecting opponents's proposals without even seeming to listen to them... The possibilities are endless.

Authority

Negotiators usually have limits on their authority to conclude an agreement. The Constitutional requirement for Senate approval of all treaties limits the authority of the President.   Purchasing agents may have separate limits on elements of contracts such as delivery time, discounts, down payments, and trade-in allowances. It is important to understand how much authority your opponents have on each component of the deal on which you are working, and to learn who can make exceptions.

Agents usually are paid a percentage of the settlement price. This works well for sellers, but not for buyers. Buyer's agents might be more appropriately motivated by a commission based on the *difference* between deadlock and settlement price. Thus, a buyers' agent would receive a larger commission for reaching a lower price. All three would have to be set carefully before negotiations began.

Limited authority may take culturally characteristic forms.   In Japan, which both frowns on direct confrontation and reaches decisions by consensus, it often leads to affirmations that others interpret as agreement when the Japanese negotiators mean only that they understood the proposal well enough to discuss it among themselves. Limited authority may be an intentional tactic to keep opponents off balance, tire them out, or provide an avenue of retreat from previous concessions. The usual technique is to pass the opponent to successively higher ranking people. At each level, the concessions made *by* the subordinate are denied, ignored or repudiated, while those made *to* the subordinate are treated as inadequate.

Children learn a variation early in life: if Mom says no, try Dad. In Juvenile Hall the technique of making the same request of repeated authorities until getting the desired permission is known as "shopping." It can of course be adapted to other circumstances. If the director of personnel says no, recast the issue appropriately and see the vice president of finance. If the vice president says no, recast it as one only the president can resolve. The basic defense is to make sure that all decision-makers know of decisions already made.

When the tactic is expected, for example in buying a car where it is almost certain, plan a two-phase negotiation. In the first phase, limit yourself to minor concessions and long-winded discussions. The early concessions must convince the opponents that agreement is possible. The discussions must be long enough for opponents to feel too much has been invested to lose the deal.

When you sense the opponents are convinced on both points, force the person with final authority into the open. Push your opponent into admitting lack of authority, then insist on talking to whoever has it. If, as sometimes happens, that individual does not really exist, the demand will lead to sudden increases in the authority of the current negotiator. If necessary, refuse further concessions, put limits on

your own authority, threaten deadlock, feign anger, or attack your opponents' importance or honesty.

A written record, sometimes signed, can be made before talking to the new negotiator. They are common in diplomatic negotiations (where they are known as *aides memoire*). They are unusual in consumer purchases--giving them potential surprise value and greater than usual power!

Do not let the new opponents summarize your concessions but not those of their own agent. Consider seizing the initiative by stating their concessions for them. If told the prior negotiator did not have the authority to make such offers, you can accuse them of bargaining in bad faith. Or, you can bring in your own higher authority (lawyer, accountant, technician, boss, or spouse, as appropriate).

Limited authority can also be used to delay a decision that may be regretted later. In this case, the individuals may not change, but the negotiations will be protracted and will involve frequent caucuses with a superior. Longer delays may be created by the superior who happens to be sick or on vacation.

Back Channels

Back channels are off-the-record, often secret, discussions outside the formal negotiating process. They often are used to overcome deadlock in sensitive circumstances, or as a face-saving device. However, their secrecy can deprive negotiators of needed technical advice, so they must be skillfully combined with the formal process if the best possible deal is to be made.

Back channels have been much used by American presidents. Wilson had Colonel House, Roosevelt had Harry Hopkins, Kennedy had McGeorge Bundy. Kissinger used them often, for example traveling secretly to China to help establish diplomatic relations. His "shuttle diplomacy" between Israel and Egypt was a semi-public back channel negotiation.

Some airlines have used the computer reservation system to post "proposed" changes in fares that really were illegal price-fixing proposals to other airlines. The affected airlines replied by sending their own "proposed" changes. The back channel need not be human!

Bad Guy/Good Guy (Mutt and Jeff)

This tactic is familiar to anyone who has ever seen a police movie. One negotiator, the bad guy, uses threats, anger, unreasonable demands, and other harsh tactics to soften up opponents. The other

negotiator, the good guy, is kind, considerate, and understanding.
He blames all the difficulties on the bad guy while seeking to obtain
concessions and agreement.

Bad guy/good guy has many variations. The good guy may pose
as your ally against his superior, who remains out of sight but over-
rules all concessions and demands more from you. This bad guy may
not even really exist! The "bad" guy may be unpleasant or merely
blunt and serious, while the "good" guy smooths matters over with a
joke or a story. The bad guy may be a group, such as a board that
must ratify any agreement. The bad guy may be a policy or law the
opponent cannot change or dares not violate.

Bad guy/good guy can be countered by protesting to the opponents
or to their superiors, by bringing in your own bad guy, or by satiriz-
ing the ploy as something from a bad movie. If the "bad guy" is a
law, rule, or policy, suggest reasons you warrant an exception, or a
different rule more favorable to your position.

Bargaining Climate

Many people dread negotiations because they dread argument.
When they must negotiate, they try to be pleasant and courteous, and
hope opponents will also. Experienced negotiators try to manipulate
the degree of cooperation, friendliness, or formality to their advantage. As it is harder to shift from animosity to cooperation than from
cooperation to animosity, most negotiations begin pleasantly.

Traditional ways to change the climate include manners good or
bad, food and drink given or withheld, and venue (discussed below).
A reputation for keeping both the letter and the spirit of agreements
can improve the bargaining climate. Small favors improve the
climate. Large ones become bribes, illegal in some cultures, expected
in others. The dividing line between the two can be a source of
confusion and difficulty, even in one's own culture. American history
has several cases of members of the Executive branch forced to resign
by members of the Legislative branch over gifts smaller than the legis-
lators themselves routinely accept.

Negotiators who hope to maintain a positive climate must control
their temper and prove they are listening carefully. Stating one's own
needs is less provocative than attacking opponents.' Trying to men-
tion something positive in an opponent's position before requesting
changes keeps everyone optimistic. In contrast, instant total rejection
often leads to accusations and arguments that undermine the bargaining climate.

Humor can change the climate either way. It can relieve tensions or build a common bond through light-hearted jokes about common problems. It also can backfire. If not used carefully, particularly in intercultural situations, humor aimed at relieving tensions can increase them instead. If you must, jokes about yourself are safest.

The bargaining climate usually changes as the negotiation progresses. Demands, argument, and rebuttal almost inevitably raise tensions. Negotiators experience sinking feelings, disappointment, frustration, and anger. Haggling (see below) is tedious, trivial, exhausting. Climate deteriorates if a negotiator suspects, even wrongly, the good faith of opponents, or is subjected to *ad hominems* or one-upmanship. Faced with such treatment, warn that you will walk out if it continues, and do so if there is no improvement. In some situations the warning gains force if it includes a threat to explain any walkout to the opponents' superior. But, the tactic will backfire if the intent of the abuse is to get the opponent to break off the negotiation.

In international negotiations where one party has flown across many time zones, it is not uncommon for the hosts to provide generous and continuous hospitality that really is aimed at exhausting the guests. In some cultures, such as Russia, endless toasts of hard liquor are customary. Magic shops have glasses that hold a fraction of what appears to be in them, a useful defense if substitution is possible.

Negotiators sometimes create, sometimes must deal with an intimidating climate. Hitler met Austrian Chancellor Schuschnigg at his Berchtesgaden retreat in February 1938. Schuschnigg, a man of impeccable manners desirous of a pleasant negotiating climate commented on the magnificent view, the fine weather, and the important meetings that had been held there. Hitler cut him short. Schuschnigg called the two-hour conversation that followed "somewhat unilateral." Hitler (Austrian by birth) fumed that Austria had contributed "absolutely zero" to German culture, that its policy was uninterrupted treason, that he would like to save it from the revenge of his storm troopers, that no country would even "raise their voice" to help Austria, that it could not resist half an hour, and that Schuschnigg had to come to terms that afternoon or else. Schuschnigg managed to ask what the terms were. Hitler snapped, "We can discuss that this afternoon." (Shirer, 1959). Hitler got what he wanted.

Ranting is not the only way to intimidate. There is a large literature on "power offices," and "dressing for success." Admiral Rickover sometimes seated job applicants in a chair with one short leg so that they were physically--and mentally--off balance through the interview. A *Wall Street Journal* cartoon shows a boss on the phone asking "There's a Harry somebody-or-other in here asking for a raise. Who the devil hired him in the first place?" Awareness of such tactics does much to thwart their effectiveness.

Bargaining climate is affected by expectations of how long the bargaining relationship will last. The tradition of courtesy to diplomats no matter how outrageously their countries behave assumes the relationship is perpetual. Salesmen treat first- or one-time customers quite differently than long-term or repeat ones. This is the real reason for the stereotype of the used car salesman as dishonest.

Bargaining Range

The bargaining range defines all offers a negotiator will make. As any offer can be accepted, every offer should be acceptable to its maker. Those who start low and concede upward are "buyers." Those who start high and concede downward are "sellers." Money need not be involved. Teens negotiating a curfew are "sellers," parents are "buyers." If their bargaining ranges overlap, there is a settlement range within which it should be possible to make a deal (Figure 2). A small settlement range suggests negotiations will be difficult but should be successful. A large settlement range suggests negotiations will be successful and relatively easy (see the discussion of Toughness below). If there is no settlement range, the negotiations will fail unless one or both parties change their goals or receive compensation on another issue.

	F O R D
Buyers' Bargaining Range	::::::::::::::::::::
Settlement Range	███████
Sellers' Bargaining Range	▓▓▓▓▓▓▓▓▓▓▓▓▓▓▓▓▓▓
	D R O F
Price	Low High

Figure 2
Bargaining and Settlement Range

Negotiators should define their bargaining range on *every* issue by First, Optimistic, Realistic, and Deadlock positions, easily remembered by the mnemonic "FORD." Setting goals significantly improves negotiating performance. This is not always easy, particularly if your side is divided (*e.g.* engineers vs. marketers, Department of State vs. Department of Defense) or the issues involve high levels of uncertainty (*e.g.* volatile currencies or unproven technologies). Determine the Deadlock position first. This is the point at which you prefer no deal, the one Fisher and Ury (1981) call the Best Alternative To A Negotiated Agreement, or BATNA, the point at which a deal does not meet your needs.

Second, assuming a worthy opponent, determine a Realistic settlement that recognizes the circumstances, needs, and power of all parties. For a plaintiff, it might be economic loss, for a college graduate's first job it might be the average starting wage for similar positions, for a warring nation that has barely held its own it might be the *status quo ante bellum*--restoration of the situation before the war.

Third, determine the most Optimistic imaginable settlement, assuming factors exist that will result in an exceptional deal whether or not you know what they are. Opponents may represent a government facing an electorate demanding peace at any price. Buyers may need the equipment to meet a deadline for their biggest customer. Sellers may have a cash flow or tax problem, or may be trying to win a monthly sales contest.

Always determine your First offer last! It cannot be so extreme that it convinces opponents no deal is possible or even insults them. A common approach is to increase the optimistic position 10-20%, but it can be selected statistically. Assume you are a seller whose best estimate of the buyers' deadlock as $5000. Treat this as the mean of a normal curve expressing the uncertainty of your estimate as the standard deviation, say $500. Specify as a percentage the risk you are willing to take of lost profit by choosing a first price below what the buyer will pay, say 5%. From a Z-table convert the risk to a Z-score (1.96 in this case), then calculate your first offer:

$$5000 + (1.96 * 500) = 5000 + 980 = 5980 = \text{First Offer}$$

Different estimates of the opponents' deadlock price, uncertainty, and attitudes toward risk will result in very different First offers.

Negotiators avoid predictable patterns to disguise their deadlock price, so divide their bargaining range into unequal segments. The Optimistic and Realistic positions provide natural points of resistance at which negotiators will slow their concession rates long enough to test opponents. This provides negotiators with one way to estimate their opponents' deadlock price.

Another way to estimate the opponents' deadlock position is to learn, or guess, what they might do without an agreement. That is, what *literally* is their BATNA? If buying a horse, know what it will fetch at the glue factory. If selling a copy machine, some idea of how much time and money the buyers are spending at the local copy shop will help you estimate their BATNA.

Some theorists define a fair bargain as the midpoint of the settlement range. Unfortunately, negotiators rarely reveal their true deadlock even after a bargain is struck, making a fair bargain so defined impossible to determine. Other theorists prefer to define a fair bargain as the midpoint between the first positions. This can be calculated but favors the negotiator with the more extreme starting position, so is heavily influenced by tactics. A more useful definition of a fair bargain is one meeting the needs of and leaving both sides better off. Therefore, *any* point within the settlement range is fair.

For example, I have five ounces of Beluga caviar and you have five ounces of foie gras, both luxury items of almost identical value ounce-for-ounce and representing the entire supply available to either of us. I love paté but cannot abide caviar. You rate them equally so prefer some of each. I suggest a straight trade--your paté for my caviar. Taking advantage of the revelation of my values inherent in the offer, you reply that you don't much like caviar (lying) but on occasion have guests who do (giving a reason to have some of it). You offer one ounce of paté for all my caviar. You will be very much better off--4 ounces of paté and 5 of caviar, while I will be somewhat better off with one ounce of something I like (and the caviar was a gift anyway). The deal is fair but unequal!

Best and Final Offer

Negotiators sometimes are asked to make their "best and final offer." This implies that the offer will be accepted or rejected without further negotiating. In practice, recipients are likely to continue negotiating just to make sure it really is "best" and really is "final."

Negotiators can respond to requests for a best and final offer in several ways. Some allow for a small final concession. Some only make no-cost concessions, such as a promise to recommend a salesman to friends. Others, not wanting a reputation for making negotiable best and final offers, will say the offer was a good faith response (implying bad faith by opponents asking for further concessions), and meant just what the term "best and final" implies. Feigned anger can stress the point. It may be worth deadlocking so future best and final offers will be taken seriously.

Negotiators sometimes identify an offer as "best and final" before one is requested. They do so to prevent opponents taking the initiative by making their own best and final offer first. Recipients of an unrequested best and final can take it seriously and accept or reject it. They can treat the offer as a concession, even complimenting opponents on a "very useful basis for further negotiation." They can change the specifications, making the offer irrelevant. Other possibilities are to ignore the offer and talk about something else, respond to an earlier proposal as if it still was on the table, request a caucus, explain what deadlock will cost opponents, feign anger, or pass the negotiations on to someone with more authority. All these tactics keep negotiations going in the face of "finality."

Better Than That

Sometimes you can get concessions simply by saying "You've got to do better than that." Unskilled or tired negotiators often assume what kind of improvement is required and make unthinking concessions. Such a concession can be accepted as helpful while explaining that was not what you required. If offered a better price, ask for faster delivery. If offered higher quality, ask for a quantity discount.

To avoid falling into the same trap, if an opponent asks you to do "better than that," first find out everything wrong with the current offer and what improvements are required. Then, either make the necessary concession and demand agreement, or explain why you cannot do so. Otherwise, your opponent will be the one "pocketing" your concession and asking for another.

A variation of this tactic is suggesting that the competition is offering a better deal, implying that your proposal must be improved if a deal is to be had. If your opponents try this, ask *what* is better about the competing offer. You are likely to learn something about your competition and something about your opponents' needs. You may learn that your opponents are bluffing. If not, you must demonstrate that your offer is the better of the two despite, or even because of, the differences.

Bluffing (Lying or "Errors")

A negotiator can bluff or lie by commission, omission, or interpretation. Bluffing is more common than, and less frowned upon, than lying, although the difference is not always easy to discern. "Errors" are a time-tested way of gaining advantage. Taxes applicable only to things can be calculated on service. Dates can be changed, "mistakes" made in arithmetic. Words that have been added, omitted, or changed can be blamed on a secretary. The price for an option can be included in the base price and as a separate item. A tax can be "forgotten" until the "error" is caught by a supervisor, when "the law" requires adding it to the price.

Bluffs and lies are common in low-trust and one-time negotiations, but the gains usually are small. They are rarer in high trust situations or long-term relations, but can have huge payoffs. Precisely because of this, negotiators must guard against bluffing and lying even in high trust situations. To give an example, a car salesman is likely to be more honest with a fleet buyer seen every year than a consumer unlikely to be seen again. But, the fleet buyer should be careful, especially if the salesman is about to change jobs or retire.

Body Language (Nonverbal Communication)

Communication involves both talking and listening. Nonverbal communication must be considered from both viewpoints.

As a way of understanding opponents, nonverbal communication probably is highly overrated. Body language is likely to be misinterpreted. A gesture may have no meaning (consciously or otherwise). Someone may take off a jacket because he is comfortable with you or because he is hot. A tense, nasal, voice may betray a lie, a cold, or a speech impediment. Changes in mannerisms probably are more significant than any particular mannerisms, but even then are easily misinterpreted.

Gestures vary in meaning among cultures, social classes or individuals. An upward jerk of the chin may mean "hello" or (as I recently discovered to my chagrin) "I want to buy drugs." You may hold your thumb and finger together in a circle meaning "OK" or give a thumbs up meaning "good" but in some countries those gestures are obscene. Axtell (1993) provides an "international gesture dictionary," necessarily incomplete but sufficient to make you careful.

As a way of influencing opponents, nonverbal communication probably is even more overrated. However, one technique that may make opponents more comfortable is imitating them in mood, posture, speech patterns (rate, tone, volume, phrases, imagery) and breathing patterns. Like every other tactic, it works sometimes but not every time. It may even backfire if the opponents think you are mocking or manipulating them. Gestures such as crossed arms that may indicate opposition, and personal characteristics such as stuttering, should *not* be imitated--unless of course deadlock is what you really are after.

Bottom Line

The bottom line refers to the final total benefits and costs of a deal. Negotiators often discuss prices in terms of units, (come down a penny each), percentage (come down .25%), or payments (come down a dollar a month). They do so to make the concession sound small and to hide a large effect on the total price. A penny each on 100,000 units is $1,000. A quarter point over the life of a mortgage can mean thousands of dollars. Always calculate the actual impact of any proposal on the bottom line on every deal. If uncertainties are involved, it often is possible to estimate the value of the deal by constructing a spread sheet for the range of possibilities and the probability of each.

Boulwarism (First and Final Offer)

This tactic takes its name from the General Electric negotiator who made his first offer his last. "First and Final Offer" fully describes the tactic. Negotiators practicing this tactic open with their deadlock price and refuse to make any concessions.

Boulwarism is a tough tactic likely to end in deadlock because it is so contrary to the expected cycle of concessions. It works only if the opponents' settlement range is known, the offer is within it, the offeror is in a very powerful position, and there are no laws that penalize the tactic. Obviously, it is rarely encountered. This gives it surprise value that might make it very effective.

Caucus

A caucus is a private meeting of the negotiators on one side. A caucus may be a brief whispered conversation at the negotiation table. It may be a private meeting of a negotiating team in a separate room (which may be bugged by opponents). Time for a caucus can be requested at any time, but long negotiations usually provide frequent natural opportunities.

Common reasons for a caucus are to review a new proposal or one with unexpected components. A caucus requested for these reasons implies a response when negotiations resume. Other reasons for a caucus are reviewing progress, reassessing opponents' or your own objectives, revising tactics, consulting with higher authority, pretending to consult with higher authority, talking with the opponents' competitors, breaking their momentum (much as is done in some sports), or sorting out confusion within the team. Obviously, do not request a caucus when opponents are making concessions, or seem to be feeling the pressure to do so.

It is possible to oppose, limit, or delay a caucus request, perhaps by pointing to a deadline. Unless the reason is sound, even if opponents remain in the room progress is unlikely, the bargaining climate is likely to deteriorate, and opponents are likely to oppose your own caucus requests. Generally, a caucus request is respected.

Closing

There is a psychological element to every agreement. Those reached too quickly may leave people feeling they could have gotten a better deal by holding out longer or by dealing with someone else. They may even feel cheated. People tend to feel best about deals they have worked to achieve. For these reasons it is unwise to conclude a deal too quickly. On the other hand, continuing to bargain when the current offer is acceptable and the opponents are ready to close risks all that has been achieved. Continuing to bargain to get every last little nugget of advantage can be an expensive mistake.

Bringing a negotiation to a successful conclusion requires knowing when to close, how to close, and how to handle opponents' closing tactics. A common mistake is to belittle remaining differences. Opponents can then logically ask you to concede what you have admitted is unimportant.

Closing attempts should be relaxed,   friendly, respectful, and confident. You must have more closings than opponents have objections. Negotiators usually prefer the least forceful, least risky closing possible.

Proposals and counter-proposals gradually bring opponents together. Readiness to close may be signaled by a shift from concerns about terms to concerns about how an agreement will be carried out, or from gaining concessions to concern that progress achieved will be lost. Despite the cautions about body language (see above), readiness to close may be signaled inadvertently by leaning back in a chair or taking a deep breath. Satisfying a major objection is an excellent time to try to close a negotiation.

Questions can be used to close. The simplest is to ask directly for agreement to your current offer. A minor variation is the two-question sequence, "Is there anything we haven't settled?" followed by "Well, then, we are agreed, right?"

Questions can be asked so they can be answered "yes" or "no," but selected so they are most likely to be answered "yes." An easy way to get into the sequence is to review what has been accomplished, or to review your understanding of opponents' needs. Whenever a "no" is encountered, the question must be revised until the opponent agrees with it. Once the opponent has said "yes" to each agenda item, finish with the two-question sequence above.

A variation is to keep asking opponents what objection they have to your offer. Dispose of each objection one at a time, ending each with "if there are no more objections I assume we have an agreement." When the opponents run out of objections, it is difficult for them to do anything but close. Difficult but not impossible. They may claim limited authority (see above) or a need to think it over (see objections, below).

Another approach is to ask questions that assume agreement. For example, in negotiating the sale of a tv, ask the prospects if they want it installed in the living room *or* the bedroom. If they choose either one, or name a third location, they are sold. The approach is even more powerful if the question incorporates a reference to some advantage to settling quickly.

Finally, be alert to requests from opponents that you can meet. Instead of simply answering yes, ask for agreement if you do meet the request. For example, if a buyer asks "If I bought this computer, would you throw in a box of floppy disks?" the seller should answer, "If I could, will you buy now?"

If you are asked questions aimed at agreement to the current proposal, you can agree! You can ignore the current proposal and respond to an earlier one (as Kennedy did during the Cuban missile crisis). You can change the subject and keep negotiating, request a caucus, or use some other closing as a counter-tactic.

Summarizing is another way to close. The simplest is summarizing everything agreed emphasizing your concessions but not theirs, then giving reasons for their agreeing to the current offer. A variation is to list all reasons for agreeing, all reasons against agreeing, and pointing out that the former outweighs latter. This is known as the "Ben Franklin close," and has become a negotiating cliche. The recipient can agree completely (closing the deal), disagree completely (risking deadlock), or specify issues on which improvement still is required, leading to further negotiation.

Offering choices is a third major approach to closing. The simplest is between two complete proposals. It is useful when the settlement range is understood (so both proposals can be made acceptable) but the relative importance of the issues is not. A Las Vegas hotel manager might offer a performer a solo performance in a lounge show seen by few or a spot in a cabaret show seen by many. A variant (known to some as the "impending doom" close) is to claim that some of the choices require immediate action: The sale ends tonight. That car will sell before you come back. Confess or die!

If the settlement range is not clear, a negotiator can offer choices that differ in price. The technique usually works best if the most likely choice is stated first (as the best for "most" people) followed by the expensive choice (as the best for a "few" people) and ending with the least expensive choice (as the best for "some" people). Thus, a computer salesman might say "Most people require the modem and dual drives on the $2495 model, a few require those features with the expanded memory and CD-ROM on the $2995 model, but some need only the features found on the $2000 model. Which of the three is closest to your budget?"

If offered choices by opponents, do not feel constrained by them. If offered a $22,000 red sedan with air conditioning or a $25,000 yellow sports car with a stereo, you might say you want the red sports car with the stereo *and* air conditioning for $23,000. Make sure your needs, not opponents' formulations of them, determine your response.

Combining the preceding methods, negotiators can ask about each decision necessary to reach agreement, record each choice in writing, and summarize the resulting progress to close. Opponents may object, so you must be ready to explain that you are writing things down to make sure you don't forget anything important to them.

Trivializing the remaining difference between parties can be effective. For example, a remaining difference of $3000 on a machine likely to be kept for three years can be translated into a weekly ($19.02), daily ($3.08) or even hourly ($.48) cost. This can be compared with some related business cost (in this case, perhaps the machine operator's wage) to ask why such a trivial difference should stand in the way of improved profitability.

Splitting the difference implies settling half way between the current proposals of each party. An aggressive negotiator can interpret an offer to "split the difference" as conceding half the difference and seek further advantage. To do so, first restate how much the opponent already has conceded. Then reject it as insufficient, preferably for a good reason. A less aggressive approach is to say you cannot afford a 50-50 split, give some strong reasons why, then wait for the response. Another possibility is to suggest a split other than 50-50, such as 80-20 in your favor, then haggle (see below).

A more subtle tactic is based on Raiffa's (1982) observation that the best prediction of a settlement point is half way between the first offers of each party, providing that point is acceptable to both. To determine the appropriate counter offer, buyers would subtract twice the difference between the sellers' offer and their own goal:

$50,000 Sellers' offer
$40,000 Buyers' goal
$10,000 Seller's offer minus buyers' goal
$30,000 Buyer's goal minus difference equals counter offer

If the mid-point between the two offers is acceptable to the sellers, they can immediately offer to split the difference. If not, they will continue to negotiate. Assuming opponents sophisticated enough to recognize the signal, the tactic is highly efficient. Obviously, sellers can make the same calculations in reverse if they receive instead of make the first offer.

The instant an offer is on the table from both parties, calculate the mid-point. If it is acceptable, it may be wise to split the difference rather than risk losing the deal or waste time trying for small advantages. If the mid-point is unacceptable, then the negotiation may fail. However, one side might get compensation on another issue, be up against a deadline, be concerned about long-term relationships, or change its goal. Circumstances may change, affecting goals during protracted negotiations or even making negotiations possible. Changing interest and employment rates affect both prices and numbers of sales of cars and houses. After years of war, the Gulf War suddenly motivated both the PLO and Israel to negotiate with one another. The PLO was in dire financial straits as a result of choosing the wrong side, and Israel realized that no occupied or demilitarized zone ever could be large enough to prevent missile attack.

Tabling issues standing in the way of agreement is a possibility. It is very common in international negotiations. It can promote agreement if at least one of three circumstances exists. First, neither side wishes to endanger progress already made. Second, resolution of the remaining issues can wait. Third, one side regards the remaining issues as non-negotiable. In the first circumstance, the delay is mutually advantageous. In the second, both sides usually believe they will get stronger with time. The third usually indicates that the negotiators' consitutents will not compromise (now) on those issues.

Tactics addressed elsewhere in this handbook provide still more ways to close. Among them are best and final offers, take it or leave it, and threats. These differ in tone. Best and final offers stress the advantages of reaching agreement. Take it or leave it implies frustration. Threats stress the costs of deadlock.

Closing a negotiation involves formalities, which can be anything from a simple "OK" to an elaborate signing ceremony. The formalities often have to await approval of the deal reached by the negotiators. Examples are the membership vote on a union contract and Senate ratification of an international treaty.

Concession Making

Negotiators must be prepared to make concessions, but must keep tabs on their rate, size, and total. Therefore, if negotiators do *nothing* else to prepare, they should at least set their deadlock. Ideally, as discussed above, they will establish a complete bargaining range on each issue. Use this range, not your opinion of your opponents (particularly in low trust situations) to evaluate proposals.

Once the bargaining range is set, plan your concession strategy. Know the importance of each concession to your own goals so you know what you must gain in return. Know how important the concession is to opponents so you know how much you can get in return. Remember that a concession is not necessarily equally important to both sides (see the discussion below of linkage). There is a very human tendency to over-value one's own concessions and under-value those of opponents. Judge concessions in terms of your goals, not in terms of who made them.

When possible, describe your concessions as gains to opponents. Don't tell buyers they are paying more, but that they are getting better quality. Don't tell sellers you are offering them less money, but saving them time. Labor negotiators can tell management that their salary proposal is necessary for a loyal, dependable work force.

Large or one-sided concessions made in hope of building goodwill are more likely to lead opponents to think you are desperate or a pigeon. Progressively smaller concessions make it easier for opponents to estimate your deadlock. Experienced negotiators vary both the size and timing of their concessions.

Concessions can be conditional to prevent them becoming one-sided. Time limits can prevent opponents delaying their response to create deadline pressure. The conditions can be firm and specific, or flexible and negotiable. A seller might offer a half-point lower interest rate conditioned on a $5000 increase in down payment. Omitting "half-point" and changing the amount to "significant" might signal that *both* are negotiable. The expiration also can be specific (a week) or ambiguous (unless another offer is received).

As the negotiation moves into the closing stage, it is important to remain alert. If you relax, sigh in relief, or allow exhaustion to cloud your judgment, opponents may try for a last minute concession, or bring up a last-minute issue and get quick concessions. Such maneuvers can be particularly effective if delivered by phone when you are thinking about everything but the negotiation.

Deadlines

The negotiator under deadline pressure usually is at a disadvantage. The Vietnamese delegates to the Paris peace talks rented a villa for a year. The Americans took hotel rooms at weekly rates. Negotiators often try to learn their opponents' deadline while concealing their own. If you are staying at a hotel, prevent opponents learning your deadline by booking a longer stay. You can always leave early.

Buyers and sellers often delay making counteroffers to put opponents under deadline pressure. Sellers often warn buyers that prices go up at the end of the month. Negotiators often give deadlines to put opponents under pressure, to protect themselves from being put under similar pressure, or to reduce opponents' opportunity to study the details of an offer.

If you are given a deadline by your opponents, you can take it seriously, conceding bargaining power. You can ignore it, gaining bargaining power if they are bluffing but making deadlock more likely if they are not. Negotiate the deadline itself, weakening opponent's to the extent that their power depends on it.

Deadlock (BATNA or Reserve Price)

Deadlock is an outcome, not a tactic. It is appropriate if bargaining ranges do not overlap to form a settlement range and compensation cannot be found on other issues. Deadlocks may also result from unfair treatment, hope for a better agreement at a later date, opponents who cannot control followers so cannot keep agreements, negotiations involving religious, ethnic, or other deeply held values and negotiations over a finite resource such as land.

Threatening deadlock is a tactic, not an outcome. It can be used when opponents fear deadlock more than concessions, so will make them to keep talks going. It is a powerful way to test opponents' resolve, but loses credibility if overused (like the boy who cried wolf). If done too abruptly, it may succeed, which is not the goal. If done too slowly, or using cliches such as slowly putting papers into a briefcase, it may be perceived as a bluff and turned on its maker.

Threatened with a deadlock, unwilling to accept the offer and desirous of reaching a settlement, delay things with a caucus (see above). Told your terms are "impossible," ask what it would take to get agreement. Ask for clarification of terms then review the entire negotiation. Point out what opponents will lose by failing to reach agreement. Ignore the threat or change the subject. Shift the discussion from specifics to broad principles and common interests. Alternatively, shift them to minor issues and procedural matters. Ask hypothetical questions about possible changes in the offer. Above all, when opponents threaten deadlock, find a way to keep talking without making concessions.

There are many ways to reopen deadlocked or move stalled negotiations. Talk off-the-record or use back channels. Change the venue. Concentrate on unimportant issues to create a sense of progress and build trust. Focus on important issues to create a sense of urgency. Divide issues into smaller ones to make each easier to settle and to increase the possibilities for tradeoffs. Decrease the number of parties to equalize power and change the alliances. Bring in new parties who can provide new ideas or resources. Increase publicity so public opinion pressures the negotiators, or decrease it so that negotiators play less to public opinion. Bring in mediators. Wait: the conflict may become too important not to settle or too trivial to warrant any effort (Kriesberg, 1989). Bring in higher ranking negotiators, or replace particular individuals. Divide and conquer. A recent example is the U.S. threat of a 200% tariff on French wine in retaliation for their intransigence on rape-seed subsidies. The possibility of a trade war divided the European Community into free trade and protectionist groups. France folded quickly.

Deadlocks create a dilemma. Negotiators should be rewarded as much for avoiding bad as for making good agreements. However, they should not be rewarded for failing to reach agreement merely because initial differences were "too large," or they failed to fully explore all possibilities, mistook tough tactics for unfair ones, or pursued unrealistic goals.

Delay

Negotiators sometimes want to slow the pace of a negotiation. They may believe that opponents' can be forced against a deadline or that their own bargaining strength will improve. They may need time to think, time to consult with others, or time to analyze proposals. Delays can be a few seconds or a few months. Negotiators trying to make opponents nervous suggest delays of uncertain duration; negotiators trying to maintain momentum want specific ones.

Negotiations can be delayed by requesting information or a caucus. They may be delayed by telling a joke, going to the bathroom, or asking for a coffee or meal break. Delays can be achieved by detailed exploration of an issue, itself important, trivial, peripheral, procedural or false. Negotiations can be delayed by filibuster, presenting "background" (beginning with Genesis), discussing precedents or regulations, or reading lengthy documents into the record. They can be delayed until a financial, legal, or technical committee, often including members selected to insure the desired outcome, can "study and report." Even the membership of the committee can be negotiated for the sole purpose of lengthening the delay. Obviously, there are ample devices to delay a negotiation for any amount of time required.

Empathy

Empathy is imagining how opponents feel. Used honestly, it improves the bargaining climate by showing that you understand and care about the opponents' problems. Used cynically (some would say skillfully), it fools opponents into thinking you care about their problems in hope they will reciprocate. Used analytically, it can increase a negotiator's power (discussed below).

Empathy begins with listening. In negotiating, that requires proving you understand opponents' positions to *their* satisfaction before presenting your own. Summarize what they said and make sure they accept your interpretation before responding. The technique is powerful in conditions of high tension or low trust. It is difficult for opponents to remain angry or assert unfair treatment in the face of efforts to understand their concerns, needs, or positions. This is half the battle.

The second half of the battle is getting opponents to reciprocate the attention given to them. You now must convince opponents to restate your position to your satisfaction before responding. This should lead to fewer interruptions and arguments. Everyone has to listen carefully if for no other reason than to avoid the embarrassment of admitting to not paying attention. Apart from the improved bargaining climate, better understanding often leads to better proposals and more satisfactory agreements.

Three other empathic techniques may prove useful. One is to eliminate barriers such as desks and to move closer (but not too close) to opponents. The second is to treat differences as a problem to be solved together using "we" and "us" instead of "me" and "you." Differences of course are blamed on a common enemy, or simply the ever-notorious "them." The third is to imitate your opponents' major perceptual mode, based on which of the senses dominates their phrasing. For example, if they often say things like "I hear you," end your offer with "How does that sound?" If they often say "I can see that," end your proposal with "How does that look?"

In negotiation, empathy is more often instrumental than genuine. But negotiators only fool themselves if they try anything less than genuine understanding of their opponents. Role reversal is a standard device for reaching an understanding of the interests underlying the claims, demands, positions, and statements of opponents. Assessing your own proposals in terms of whatever personal, financial, strategic, policy, and similar consequences they may have for your opponents is exceptionally useful.

Face Saving

Skilled negotiators try to make it easy for both opponents and themselves to make concessions. They avoid early commitment to firm positions, ask opponents for "changes" instead of concessions, or provide them with some good reason, such as new information, for conceding. Other devices that negotiators use to save face or help opponents do so are reviewing the assumptions on which offers are based, raising new issues, linking two previously unrelated issues, and statements combining firmness on one element (perhaps cost) with

ambiguity on another (perhaps delivery date).   In the event cost
concessions cannot be obtained, it can then be blamed or credited as
needed on the final delivery date.

Skilled negotiators never allow opponents to learn they could have
won more concessions, even after agreement is reached. They do not
want to make future negotiations tougher. Instead, they complement
opponents on driving a hard bargain or getting the best of the deal.
They make their own concessions grudgingly even when surrendering
a straw man, and give opponents ways to explain to their own superiors why greater concessions were impossible or risky.

Good and Bad Faith (Surface Bargaining)

Negotiators do not always want to resolve disagreements. That is,
they may negotiate in bad faith.   Milner's negotiations with Kruger
were mentioned in the introduction. There is no more famous example than Hitler at Munich. Sadaam Hussein provides a recent example.   Marxist-Leninist doctrine specifically treats negotiation as a
tactic along with infiltration of protest movements, strikes, terrorism,
propaganda, guerrilla and conventional war in "wars of national liber-
ation." The tactics are used cyclically to achieve legitimacy, gain a
share of power, then win control of the government. Thus, those who
advocate negotiation with groups such as the Sandinistas only demonstrate own naivete. It is unwise to automatically assume opponents
share your values, ethical codes, and intentions.

Bad faith bargaining is the subject of much U.S. labor law. One
definition is "generally implying or involving actual or constructive
fraud, or a design to mislead or deceive another, or a neglect or
refusal to fulfill some duty or contractual obligation, not prompted by
an honest mistake as to one's rights or duties but by some interested
or sinister motive (*Black's Law Dictionary*, 1968: State v. Griffin,
100, SC 331 84 SE 876, 877)."

Surface bargaining (bargaining without intent to reach agreement),
reneging on concessions, predicating settlement on surrender of statu-
tory rights, and assigning negotiators with no authority are widely but
not universally recognized as bad faith tactics.   It can be hard to
detect the point at which a tough but fair tactic such as the Sibylline
Books becomes an unfair one such as bait and switch. Opponents are
not bargaining in bad faith simply because they have not made a
concession as readily as hoped, or because an offer is completely
unrealistic. They are not bargaining in bad faith simply because they
interpret facts differently, provide only partial answers to questions,
or do not explain their feelings about objective facts.

Good faith negotiation is recognized by general adherence to the process described in the introduction and the section on concessions. Within that framework there is great latitude for skill and imagination.

Negotiators sometimes try to soften opponents' positions by accusing them of bargaining in bad faith. Accusing opponents who view their tactics as fair can undermine the bargaining climate (see above). Accusing opponents who are trying to frustrate you can prove to them that their tactics are succeeding. On the other hand, negotiators who fail to object to unethical tactics take the risk of appearing too weak to protect their own interests, a situation likely to lead to deadlock if false and to disadvantageous agreements if true. Problems are most likely when opponents are from different cultures, social classes, or professions.

Haggling

Haggling consists of alternating concessions until agreement or deadlock is reached. Haggling is almost exclusively the form of bargaining found in swap meets, street markets, and oriental bazaars, where it may be as much ritual as negotiation. It can be important in settling small differences during the closing phase of major negotiations.

Haggling is a simple process, with settlement usually about half way between the first offers of each party. Haggling puts the negotiator making the first offer at a disadvantage (see "splitting the difference" under closing tactics, above). Thus, haggling often is preceded by verbal fencing to maneuver the opponent into making the first offer.

If you cannot trap your opponents into making the first offer, determine if the half-way point between the first two offers is acceptable. If not, try to gain compensation on another issue (see Linkage) or consider immediate deadlock.

If trapped into making the first offer with no idea what the price should be (a common problem for tourists with no idea of local prices) offer the local equivalent of a penny with a laugh to make clear it is a joke. If this smokes out an offer no more than double what you are willing to pay, immediately implement the "split the difference" close (see above). If not, withdraw courteously (which may smoke out a reasonable offer).

Ignorance

Negotiators often want to prove their skills and knowledge to their opponents. But, feigning ignorance can be a good way to obtain useful or unintended explanations, gain time to think and, pushed to the extreme, drive opponents to real, exploitable anger. It is a favorite tactic among women dealing with men. The tactic can be countered by insisting that opponents clarify their questions so that you can answer them, or by the information tactics discussed immediately below.

Tactical ignorance should not be confused with real ignorance. The unprepared negotiator is at the mercy of the opponent. The ignorant usually make bad deals and never know it!

Information

Negotiations often involve information disparities among the parties. Sellers, whether of cars or companies, usually know more than buyers. This is not always the case. For example, heirs selling an estate to professional auctioneers usually know less than the buyers. In some cases, particularly mergers, all parties may be faced with information disparities. Negotiators facing such an asymmetry can request a warranty. They can rely on a knowledgeable, neutral third party to authenticate the opponents' claims. Most powerful of all, particularly in negotiations involving uncertainties such as developing technologies or future sales, they can make conditional agreements.

Information can be sought, withheld or given. It can be partial or complete, true or false. Tactics to verify information or test assumptions include ignorance (see above), listening, objections, and questions (see below), or turning to independent sources.

The appropriate sources depend on what is being negotiated. Possibilities include the Internet, computer data bases such as Nexus, information services such as Dunn & Bradstreet, libraries, public records, newspapers, professional societies, government studies, and annual reports. Colleagues, friends, and enemies of opponents may have valuable information. Spies can be hired; traitors can be bought. Allow sufficient time and money during the preparation phase, or use delay tactics during the bargaining phase, to find, collect, organize, and assess information.

During the exploration phase, focus on learning opponents' needs and the relative priorities among those needs. Try to learn how important the current negotiations are to their overall goals, and who else they might deal with if not with you. Remember that opponents will be assessing you in the same way. Know in advance what you will and will not let them know. Do not give up bargaining power by letting opponents know time constraints, financial, or other weaknesses or, sometimes, strengths. If you are trying to buy property for $900,000, do not let the seller know that you can borrow $1,000,000.

There is a fine line between giving opponents enough information to make useful offers and giving them information they can use against you. Both sides face the same dilemma, so negotiators usually exchange rather than give away information.

Although the usual strategy is to reveal information gradually, reversing the norm can work. Put forth in the guise of being open and cooperative, it can improve the bargaining climate. A full disclosure of your problems sometimes wins the sympathy of the opponents or (more likely and more usefully) involves them in developing creative and mutually advantageous solutions. The tactic is more likely among professional negotiators representing absent clients.

A perverse way of limiting the opponents' information is to overwhelm them with more information than they can possibly analyze and interpret. This "snow job" should be as voluminous, technical, trivial, and disorganized as possible. It can contain errors and contradictions. Questions should be answered by referring opponents to the information provided. This often results in confused opponents poking about in the data for a short time then giving up. Faced with this tactic, ask for the specific references that answer *each* question, then for a caucus to review them.

Another approach to providing information is to call on an expert--or someone who appears to be one. Sometimes, real knowledge may be less important than self-confidence and glibness. Faced with an expert, verify his credentials, then call in your own, preferably of greater age, number of degrees, publications, ability, reputation, and glibness. Another approach to dealing with opponents' experts is to broaden the discussion to issues outside their expertise.

Negotiators sometimes intentionally give poor or distracting information. They might try illogical statements, straw men (see below) complicated technical or financial details, statistics, or multiple offers, then discuss them simultaneously and erratically. The tactic can be used in the Exploration Phase to test the opponents' preparation. In the Bargaining Phase it can lure them into mistakes. In the Closing phase, distracting information can divert attention from issues you want to avoid, or induce tired opponents to agree without thinking through the implications of all the new information.

Distractions or poor information can be countered by insistence on adhering to the agenda, taking each proposal in turn, or asking detailed questions about each. If the proposals were introduced primarily to confuse, they probably have no substance and will be withdrawn quickly when tested seriously.

Linkage (Log rolling, Tie-ins or Tradeoff)

Consider the two-issue, two-party negotiation in Figure 3. If the parties split the difference on each issue, both will have $1.50, and the joint gain will total $3. If instead the parties link the issues, each making a complete concession on the issue it rates less valuable, both parties will have $2, a 33% increase in value for *both* parties, and the joint gain is $4.

The example illustrates linkage reduced to the simplest case. Linkage requires negotiators who value two or more issues differently. In that circumstance, it is possible to "make the pie" bigger" or in the language of Lax and Sebenius (1986) to "create value." The more issues there are, the greater the number of possible linkages. Therefore, complicating the agenda by adding or subdividing issues may increases chances for a agreement! Of course, as any baseball card trader knows, exchanges need not always be one-for-one.

	Issue A	Issue B
Value to negotiator one	$2	$1
Value to negotiator two	$1	$2
Total	$3	$3

Figure 3
Two-issue, Two-party Negotiation

Once negotiators learn that their relative priorities differ, it becomes possible to fashion a mutually advantageous solution. Linkage can involve intangible issues such as appearance, precedent, prestige, and tradition. Form can be traded for substance. But, the most common tradeoffs are among cost, quality, and time. The basic technique is to offer large concessions on low priority items to obtain large concessions from opponents on items of high importance to themselves. It works best when priorities differ among opponents.

An important variation is to use a third issue to link issues important to each negotiation. If one party most values reduced cost, the other time, concentrate on adjusting quality. Reduce the scope of services, use cheaper materials, sacrifice appearance but not function. If one party values time and the other quality, concentrate on adjusting cost. Buy or sell in volume, adjust delivery time to price, hire extra workers to complete the project sooner. If one party values quality and the other values cost, concentrate on adjusting time. Change the project deadline or get a loan to buy the needed quality.

The economist Vilfredo Pareto proved that a curve could be calculated that encloses all possible outcomes of a negotiation. The curve itself marks the maximum value possible in any negotiation. Continuing the example of Figure 3, the corner of the shaded area in Figure 4 marks the $1.50 each party receives by splitting the difference on both issues. Concessions that move horizontally or vertically toward the curve improve the position of one party without hurting the other. Moving diagonally toward the curve benefits both parties. Once the curve is reached, further improvement is impossible. Further gains can only be made at the expense of the opponents, the characteristics Lax and Sebenius (1986) call "claiming value."

Calculating the Pareto Optimal Frontier, the "ideal" set of agreements to every negotiation, requires differentiating utility functions for each negotiator. However, negotiators seldom reveal their utilities to one another, making the calculation impossible in most cases. Instead, negotiators usually must estimate it by subsequent approximation. An efficient process for doing so is to offer pairs of proposals, basing each subsequent pair on whichever one of the prior two the opponent indicates is more promising.

Brooks (Spring 1994) points out that linkage is particularly effective in highly adversarial negotiations because each side wins on one issue. Further, he says, if you always win on every issue, you are unlikely to like the replacement your opponents send in.

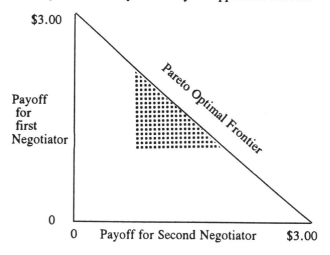

Figure 4
Pareto Optimal Frontier

Listening

People think listening is easy because it does not seem to require doing anything. It isn't easy and few people do it well. They drift into their own thoughts, hearing only part of what others say. They remember only part of that. They misinterpret much of what they remember. They miss important points and concentrate on inconsequential ones. Signals suggesting ways to resolve differences often go unnoticed.

Listening means more than not talking. It requires concentrating on what opponents say. It means letting them know you are listening carefully by taking notes or looking at them while they speak (avoid any gestures or expressions suggesting agreement or disagreement). Listening requires evaluating what opponents say. Are they right? Are they bluffing or lying? Have they contradicted themselves? How do they *feel* about what they are saying? Are they signaling needs, possible concessions or linkages, or concerns? Are opponents drawing out their remarks to build acceptance time or reduce your aspirations? Sinking feelings, disappointment, or anger *before* hearing an offer warn this tactic may be in play.

There is a cliche: you can't lose a negotiation while the opponent is talking. Interruptions irritate opponents or, worse, may prevent them making a concession or a revelation. They deprive you of information. Don't interrupt out of impatience. If you do, choose anger or apology to match your purpose. The impact will be greater.

Objections

Negotiators raise objections to obtain concessions, test resolve, or signal needs. Negotiators might object to the agenda or the venue. They might object to the accuracy or relevancy of an opponents' facts, or the interpretation or conclusions drawn from them. They may object to the opponents' tactics or even the makeup of their team. Negotiators can object to the product, terms, service, or any other part of an agreement.

Opponents make objections too, so negotiators must be able to defend as well as attack. Some objections are ambiguous, intentionally or not. "My people won't like that" could refer to price, delivery time, procedure, or color. "People" could refer to superiors, subordinates, colleagues, stock holders, or customers. Assuming the statement refers to price may lead a negotiator to offer a concession the opponents will "pocket," then tell you what they really want. Make sure you understand an objection before responding. If caught in this trap, give opponents a choice between the previous concession and the one they are requesting as a way of taking the former back.

Make sure you understand an objection before responding to it. Objections signaling real needs must be addressed if any deal is to be reached. Objections made to test your resolve need not be. Objections made to extract concessions can be met by asking first whether meeting them guarantees completion of the deal.

Some objections can be ignored, glossed over as a joke, or turned on their maker. Others can be turned to advantage, "turning lemons into lemonade." If opponents object to an obsolete component, point to its reliability. If they raise numerous objections, express surprise that they did not go to a competitor. Opponents then have to explain why they want to deal with you, taking the sting out of their own objections. Those based on assumptions (the inflation rate), interpretation (the importance of inflation to the deal), or error (the preliminary inflation rate has been corrected) can be debated.

Some negotiators, especially salesmen, hear the same objections over and over. They should prepare convincing rebuttals to each and have documentation instantly available. This is more powerful than a verbal claim. All negotiators have said, or heard, "I'll think it over." Treat this as an objection. Ask if the opponents are just trying to get rid of you. If they are polite and say no, ask for an assurance that they will give your proposal serious consideration. If they remain polite and say they will, ask them what it is about your proposal they want to think over. Make a mental or written note, and keep asking for additional objections until assured there are no others. That makes it harder for them to raise a new objection later. Now, everything depends on your ability to eliminate each objection.

One-text Procedure

In describing the Camp David negotiations, President Carter said at the National Conference on Peace and Conflict Resolution in 1991 "To be very frank about it, Sadat was almost completely accommodating. Prime Minister Begin was the most reluctant member of the Israeli delegation. But, we prepared a single text document, well known in theory, that was moved back and forth between the two men, and eventually reached agreement."

The one-text procedure involves preparation of a draft agreement, clearly labeled as such, incorporating as many points of agreement as possible. Each party revises it in turn, explaining the reasons for changes made. Alternatively, a mediator or other third party can prepare successive revisions. Ideally, each successive draft will be slightly more acceptable to all parties, and the text eventually will become the agreement itself.

The one-text procedure can minimize the continual rehashing of the same arguments without progress toward agreement. It is useful where distance makes it difficult for negotiators to get together, and has been made easier by faxes and electronic mail. People who write better than they speak under pressure may prefer it, as might those who require a historical record of a negotiation. The one-text procedure can be very useful in low-trust, high-tension negotiations. People usually are more careful writing than speaking. The one-text procedure gives them a chance to cool down, review, and revise before responding. Writing encourages brief, pertinent replies.

When mediators are involved, the one-text procedure helps negotiators deny responsibility for concessions. One explanation given for the failure of the Madrid peace talks was United States refusal to accept authorship for the concessions so that the Israeli delegation could claim they had to agree to them to maintain good relations with the United States.

Patience and Perseverance

Hasty agreements often leave negotiators with the uneasy feeling that additional concessions could have been gained or that some issues were overlooked. Out-waiting opponents lowers their expectations and separates what they want from what they need. Creative solutions require time to emerge.

Simply out-waiting opponents may lead to concessions. Perseverance--sometimes simply endlessly repeating the same proposal--can wear opponents down. Perseverance requires toughness, even insensitivity. The tactic has earned Russian, Chinese, North Korean, and Vietnamese negotiators grudging admiration.   Overused, it reduces trust; carried to extremes, it risks deadlock or charges of bad faith. Therefore, it probably is best employed in one-time negotiations or when opponents cannot deal with anyone else.

Faced with such opponents, their perseverance must be undermined. One way is to "kill them with kindness." Have one team negotiate with them all day and a second entertain them all night. Jet-lagged negotiators deprived of sleep, suffering from too little or too much food or drink, and under pressure from home to get a deal are especially likely to make mistakes.   The longer and more important the negotiations, the more attention should be given to insuring negotiators get regular meals, regular rest, and regular relaxation.

Persuasion

As Adam Smith observed, "It is not from the benevolence of the butcher, the brewer or the baker that we expect our dinner, but from their regard to their own interest." Opponents must be persuaded that your proposals meet their needs, not yours. Therefore, persuasion begins by listening. Some people want to save money, some to save time, some to save--or avoid--work. Some want to be in the know, some to be in style. Some seek prestige, power, or security.

Once opponents' needs are understood, you must find ways to meet them. Tell the buyer worried about getting production going quickly about fast setup and short training time. Tell the buyer worried about declining profits about improved productivity. Offer inexpensive upgrades or liberal trade-ins to the buyer worried about obsolescence.

When opponents resist your ideas, the natural thing is to argue. Detecting and countering alogical or illogical arguments or determining whether facts and statistics should be accepted are well beyond the scope of this book. Much has been written on both. Fischer's *Historians' Fallacies* and Katzer's *Evaluating Information* complement one another. The danger is an argument over who is "right," which may delay or even prevent settlement. Of course, it always is possible to start an argument for exactly this purpose!

If, however, you are more interested in winning the agreement than winning the argument, find out how your offer falls short. Change tactics if the issue must be settled immediately and change topics if the dispute can be settled later. Differences that do not hinder agreement often can be ignored.

Pitch language, manner, and voice to situation. Even a good case can be lost by a speaker who is condescending, insulting, or arrogant. Weak or strong, a case can be improved by a speaker who is courteous, competent, credible, enthusiastic, sincere, and witty.

Speakers often begin with jokes or stories. In a negotiation, well-timed, well-selected, jokes can break the ice, relieve tension, and help draw people together. But, people take jokes in unpredictable ways, sometimes interpreting them as personal insults or as making light of their concerns. Too many undermine credibility.

Negotiators usually make a better beginning by reviewing common interests, progress made toward agreement, the advantages of reaching agreement, the disadvantages of not reaching agreement, or all four. They may present evidence, positions and proposals. Evidence includes comparisons, examples, expert opinion, facts, reports, and statistics. Positions can involve evidence, methods, opinions, and reasons. A persuasive way to present a proposal is benefits first, features second, price third, and terms last.

Power

Power is positive or negative, the ability to reward or punish, to influence whether others act or do not. Power is as much perception

as reality, and perceptions can be changed. Two parties were negotiating a large international financial venture in Africa. One team
provided the political contacts, necessary for success, but consisted of
two people in a startup company that would go under without the
deal. The other team provided the financial contacts. It was larger,
established, and secure. An impasse developed over $150,000, one-
seventh of one percent of the total deal. The real issue was power.
When everyone was comfortably settled at the table again the weaker
of the two principals said, "I would like to speak to your CEO alone.
Everyone else please leave the room now." The impasse was quickly
broken. More important, members of the larger team realized that
the two principals were the only ones who mattered.

Negotiators must assess the sources and extent of their own power
compared to their opponents, and use it accordingly. Power has many
forms. Ten, alphabetically, are:

Audacity is power. As the anecdote above suggests, willingness
to take risks varies both with personality and with situation.

Charisma in its many but often fleeting forms (charm, fanaticism,
prestige, single-mindedness) is power. Reagan survived Irangate and
Nixon was destroyed by Watergate partly because the former was, but
the latter was not, likable.

Image is power. President Carter was weak partly because he
seemed uncomfortable with and unlikely to use power. President
Reagan was strong partly because he seemed comfortable with so
likely to use power and kept people guessing when and how he would
do so.

Knowledge is power. It takes many forms, *e.g.*, analytical,
circumstantial, creative, experiential, financial, intellectual, legal,
moral, practical, and technical. The old sergeant who knows the
informal workings of the army has power undreamt of by the new
lieutenant who outranks him on paper.

Legitimacy is power. Legitimacy can come from position, such as
boss, judge, owner, priest, or teacher. It can come from custom,
industry standards, laws, precedents (see below), published price lists,
or veto power, among many possibilities.

Options increase power. The more ways that negotiators have to
achieve their goal, the less they fear deadlock. The country with
boycott, covert action, embargo, financial and military options is
stronger than one entirely dependent on terrorism. A car buyer in a
city with many dealers and good public transportation has more power
than a buyer in a small town with one dealer and no bus service.

Ruthlessness is power. Lyndon Johnson bullied opponents. Hitler and Stalin killed them.

Time is power. Knowing an opponent's deadline increases the power of a negotiator who has or can pretend to a later one. Power often changes over time because needs and circumstances change. Therefore, the ability to wait can be power.

Trustworthiness is power. It comes from a reputation for candor, credibility, honesty, integrity, and carrying out both promises and threats.

Understanding is power. Understanding one's own goals is essential. Power increases with understanding of the opponent's costs and benefits, desires, needs, and power.

Weaker negotiators can try combinations of tactics such as arranging an advantageous agenda, bluffing, changing the venue, delaying the negotiations or reverse auctions. They can try flattery, decreasing or increasing the number of parties or issues, dividing opponents against one another, stressing common interests with factions among opponents to get them bargaining against themselves, or throwing themselves on the mercy of their opponents.

The weaker party can analyze the situation from their opponents' perspective. Any particular negotiation is likely to be more important to the weaker party, so it will command more of their talent and attention. Consider the Soviet negotiations with Egypt in the Nasser era. The Soviets certainly were the stronger of the two parties, but they were engaged on many fronts. They needed a quick resolution so moved quickly to their deadlock position when faced with a determined Egypt. Similarly, a new employee is concerned mainly with compensation and a few related issues; the employer has to get *someone* hired and keep the entire business going as well.

The weaker party can reassess the sources of their power to find new ideas, leverage, or options. Hitler was willing to negotiate with a completely defeated France in 1940 because the French fleet might sail to British ports and DeGaulle might set up a government in exile (which he did anyway, but the existence of Vichy kept its legitimacy in question). In an undoubtedly apocryphal story, a prisoner maintained his supply of cigarettes by threatening to bloody his head against the cell wall and claim the guard was abusing him.

The weaker party should search for parties with whom it can make alliances. This does not just apply in international diplomacy. Sellers form cartels, buyers form cooperatives, and bureaucrats "network" in ways often called "Byzantine" for their complexity.

Opponents can be presented with a *fait accompli*. At our university, a colleague wanted to paint her office purple and cream. Knowing they were not among the four permitted colors, and that chances for approval of an exception were nil, she came in one weekend and painted her office as she wanted (it looked better than it sounds, particularly compared with the authorized ones). Needless to say, it stayed that way, nor were there any repercussions.

A final caution. Most negotiations involve mutual needs and most negotiators have an alternative if they feel demeaned, or will get their revenge later. Therefore, specific power is more important than general power. Using as little power as possible is the most effective in the long run.

Precedent

Negotiators sometimes say that they could not possibly meet opponents' demands because they would have to make the same concession to everyone else. The assertion is powerful when it can be proven, is widely believed, or when it is difficult to verify or refute.

Four counter-tactics are possible. The first is a series of questions. Start by making sure opponents are serious about precedents. Then ask how they keep track of them, and then for a list of all precedents affecting you. If done quickly, opponents are likely to see the trap. If interspersed among other points, opponents will be placed in the position of bargaining in bad faith if the request is not met when the trap is sprung. It must be done carefully to prevent deterioration of the bargaining climate.

A better counter-tactic is to name features of the current deal that put it outside those covered by the precedent. This provides opponents with a face-saving way to make concessions. A third counter-tactic is to find out and make sure you are getting the same terms given others. The final counter-tactic is to use linkage to obtain concessions on other issues.

Preconditions

Preconditions often are an effort to obtain advantage even before negotiations start. At the least, negotiators want to avoid beginning at a disadvantage. Preconditions that often are settled before negotiations begin include the agenda (see above) and the venue (see below). Physical conditions, including such details as symbols of authority, chairs of equal height and comfort, and even table shape, have been the subject of preconditions. The number, status, and rank of the negotiators on each team, official language, media relations, and the use of experts might be important (see preparation, above). Use of tape recorders, release of information to the media, and responsibility for record-keeping may also be preconditions to negotiations.

Proposals

Agreements are reached by suggesting, defending, and modifying proposals. Ostensibly, a proposal suggests a specific way to resolve one or more issues. They can serve other purposes, such as conveying determination or trying to reduce the opponents' aspirations. Ambiguous proposals can be made to prevent deadlock by giving the parties something to talk about. They can be made to win public sympathy, prove loyalty to constituents or revive their hopes, or to make opponents look unreasonable.

Negotiators accomplish these purposes by tone and phrasing. Proposals described as suggestions, demands, or ultimatums have very different impacts. Proposals can be sufficiently attractive to generate interest but sufficiently ambiguous to encourage questions. Ambiguity makes face saving changes, replacements, or withdrawals easy. Proposals aimed more at mollifying constituents or the public than reaching agreement often contain popular principles (such as the "level playing field" in international trade) but few specifics. Ambiguous proposals may come from opponents who are poorly prepared, unskilled, or have read this book.

It is psychologically difficult to shift from the exploratory to the bargaining phase. Most people are at least a trifle embarrassed at making an offer they know is absurd. Therefore, novice negotiators often make tentative opening proposals. This is a mistake, inconsistent with the accompanying explanations about how fair, rational, and serious the proposal is (which it probably isn't). Opponents will sense the uncertainty and understand that you have left plenty of bargaining room. Make opening proposals with *chutzpah*.

Opponents' proposals can be accepted, ignored, laughed off, questioned, or rejected. You can request explanations, justifications, modifications, or time to consider them. Consider the impact of each on the bargaining climate (see above) when choosing among them.

Proposals always include an offer and may include concessions (discussed above), conditions, or a time limit. Offers can be firm and specific, such as one to buy a yacht for $300,000, half down, the balance in 24 monthly payments. A firm offer can be made to tie down a concession offered by the opponents, or to test the firmness of their position. Offers can be tentative or ambiguous, such as one to "work on reducing the interest rate to make the payments more manageable." This proposal does not guarantee a reduction, does not say how much the reduction will be, and is ambiguous about what is considered "manageable." An ambiguous offer is one way to keep talks going without making a concession.

Conditions provide a way to insure that concessions are recipro-cated. They too can be specific or ambiguous. A quarter point reduc-tion in the interest rate might be conditioned on a $5000 increase in the down payment. Offering a "significant improvement" in the interest rate for a "larger" down payment makes both the concession and the condition ambiguous, therefore negotiable.

Time limits are important in at least three circumstances. One is when negotiators are agents and deals must be ratified. Another is when your proposal depends on current conditions such as existing interesting rates or technology. The last is when a delayed response will push you against a deadline.

Questions and Answers

Negotiators do not ask or answer questions out of curiosity or desire to instruct, but to reach favorable agreements. Questions have four main purposes. The most straightforward and most common is to obtain information. Questions that help determine opponents' absolute and relative priorities enable you to improve your own proposals. Examples are "Which of these possibilities is most im-portant to you?" "If you could only have one of the three options, which would it be?" "How would you decide?" "What would make the proposal acceptable?"

Second, questions can give information. Asking where a property is located gives no information; asking how far it is from a school suggests a need. Third, questions such as "are we ready for the next issue?" aim at keeping the negotiation moving. Finally, questions can challenge facts and assumptions without attacking opponents. "Can we review the allowances for inflation?" is less confrontational than "Inflation never will be as high as you assume!"

Questions can be general or specific. They usually become more specific as a negotiation proceeds. General questions are useful for conveying or identifying needs. Specific questions asked early may miss the mark and reveal information prematurely. General questions asked late risk opening new issues, may suggest inattention to earlier answers, and are less likely to move the negotiation toward a close.

Questions can be phrased to give opponents as much or as little latitude in answering as desired. "What kind of home do you want?" gives buyers freedom to talk about size, location, style, or anything they think important. Leading questions such as "Are you ready to look at the kitchen now?" limit opponents' choices. Rhetorical questions such as "Doesn't everyone know that rising interest rates mean houses are not selling very fast these days?" are intended to give, not get, information.

Questions usually are asked singly, but they can be asked in rapid succession, without giving the opponent a chance to answer. This technique, which takes practice, maintains control and is used to lead an opponent to accept your conclusion.

When answering questions, many negotiators are cursed with having been good students. They try to answer clearly and completely, and are afraid to look stupid. Politicians provide a better model. They know which questions to answer, which questions to avoid. Politicians know when to be clear, when to be ambiguous, when to omit, when to distort, and when to bluff. They answer questions that were not asked, or rephrase the question then answer their own version. Sometimes they give a reason for not answering, promise the information later, or simply say they can't answer. They repeat previous answers or answer only part of the question. "Professor" Irwin Corey carried the technique to the extreme when asked "Why do you wear tennis shoes?" He said that was two questions, "Why?" and "Do you wear tennis shoes." He gave a ten-minute answer to the first question that left no one the wiser and never addressed the "second" question. Learn from instead of getting mad at people who use these techniques. They are useful to negotiators.

Summaries are useful to insure that all parties understand things the same way, or to synthesize complex presentations. They can get a negotiation moving that has bogged down in repetition or can slow down a negotiation that is moving too fast.

Raisin Picking (Cherry Picking)

Just as children sometimes "pick raisins out of the pudding," or shoppers pick through the cherries to get the ripe ones, buyers sometimes buy components from several sellers. They begin by obtaining detailed bids from competitors, then choose one of two approaches.

The first approach is to buy each component from the supplier who offers it most cheaply, then assemble the components themselves. Many shoppers use this approach, going from store to store to get each item they need at the most favorable price. Unless they are careful or know what they are doing, they may lose more in time and travel costs than they gain by the effort. In complex products, components from several sources may not function well together.

The second approach is to use the lowest bid on each component as the basis for further negotiations. This avoids the disadvantages of the first approach. It puts sellers on the defensive, forcing them to explain why their prices are higher on some items. Even if it does not result in a price reduction, it is very likely to obtain explanations about the product or service, or information useful in choosing among competitors.

Reverse Auction (Bellyup Negotiation)

The reverse auction is useful in buying complicated but poorly understood products or services. Buyers may not understand what the issues are, what questions should be asked, or what options are open to them. In a reverse auction, sellers are told who they are bidding against. This encourages each bidder to offer the best possible price. More important, it encourages them to explain the advantages of their own and the disadvantages of the competitors' product. The information gained can be used to revise the specifications before inviting new bids.

Faced with a reverse auction, try to bid last. Ask for an opportunity to respond to competitors' bids. Convince opponents you are willing to learn and meet their needs. Once understood, explain how your product or service is better than the competition in meeting their needs. Knowing that the competition will point out the weaknesses of your product, prove that they are irrelevant to the buyers' needs.

Salami Slicing (Nibble, Nickel and Dime, One Step at a Time)

Salami slicing, from the way butchers slice meat to fill a sandwich at lowest cost, describes asking for small concessions one after another. Salami slicing is a way to make progress under conditions of low trust. The tactic works best if begun with issues of low importance to the opponents.

Salami slicing may be useful early in a negotiation against opponents facing a deadline. The progress made makes it unlikely they will turn to a competitor, while the time it is taking may force major concessions as they run out of time.

Salami slicing becomes nibbling or nickling and diming when the request includes the threat of backing out of the deal. The classic case is asking for a free necktie after the tailor has taken the measurements for the suit and written the bill. Other nibbles are requesting extra service, free advice, gift wrapping, express delivery, free alterations, improved packaging, or extra manuals. Sellers are nibbling when they suggest accessories or an extended warranty as the sales slip is being prepared.

The usual tactics (discussed elsewhere) for defeating salami slicing include publishing prices, denying authority to make the concession, treating the request as a joke, ignoring it, or takebacks. If the nibble is expected, its value can be included in the offer or suggested before the buyer does. It is difficult to say you don't need a tie and a few minutes later threaten not to buy the suit unless a free tie is provided. The buyer too has invested time and effort in the deal, and is unlikely to go through the whole process again for so small a benefit.

Sibylline Books (Lowball or Takeback)

In Roman mythology, Sibyl offered nine books of prophecies to King Tarquin. Tarquin offered a lower price, which Sibyl answered by burning three of the books. She then offered the remaining six at the original price. Tarquin protested at paying the price for nine books when only six remained. Sibyl's answer was to burn three more and offer the remaining three at the original price. Tarquin paid the price asked for all nine to get the surviving three (Bullfinch, 1970: XXXII). Her tactic makes Boulwarism (see above) seem mild.

Negotiators expect opponents to begin with extreme positions then make concessions narrowing the gap until agreement is reached. It is possible instead to follow Sibyl's practice. Product destruction is rare. The usual method is to make a very attractive first offer (lowball). Buyers then must be convinced that they need accessories, a higher priced model, instruction, a warranty, or almost anything else that will raise the profit. A variant is to argue that conditions, for example interest rates, have changed during the negotiations and require an adjustment in the original offer. Another is to invalidate a previous concession on the basis of an opponent's failure to meet conditions attached to it. Buyers can use the tactic too. For example, home buyers can use problems found during the inspection period to justify reducing their offer.

This tactic sometimes degenerates into "bait and switch," often illegal and certainly unethical. Bait and switch involves offering "limited quantities" of non-existent items at unbelievably low prices. Customers then are told that the model offered is sold out but another model is available at the regular price. Buyers can bait and switch too, by making a token deposit, waiting till the seller is up against a deadline, then threatening to back out unless the price is reduced. Buyers may have legal recourse against bait and switch, but sellers protect themselves best by large non-refundable deposits.

The takeback is useful against nibbling and ambiguous objections. It diverts opponents' attention from getting small concessions to restoring those they already had counted on. It signals opponents that they better worry more about averting deadlock than small advantages. Head off charges of bad faith bargaining by pointing out that the nibble or objection itself raises new issues justifying the takeback.

Signals

A signal is wonderfully flexible. It can hint at a direction or topic for discussion or the contents of a proposal. It can imply willingness to make concessions, areas in which concessions might be offered or are desired, or both. A signal can suggest that lack of progress is endangering success. It should be ambiguous enough that it can be disavowed if it does not work. Therefore, leaks, spokesmen whose authority can be denied, and ambiguous actions or statements are classic ways to send signals.

A signal can be a condition, a qualification, a suggestion, or an action. Responding to issues in a different order may signal (intentionally or not) that opponents value them differently, opening linkage possibilities. Calling something impossible is not a signal, calling it improbable or possible may be. Calling quality non-negotiable may signal that price is. Specifying the delivery date and price together may signal money can be saved by later delivery or earlier delivery guaranteed for a higher price. Explaining options, warranties, licensing, and similar items may signal ways to change price. Putting papers in a briefcase to signal proximate deadlock has become a negotiating cliche.

A set of signals used so often that little ambiguity remains revolves around diplomatic recognition. Withholding recognition signals doubts about a government's legitimacy, disapproval of its policies, or even the wish for its downfall. Other signals more-or-less in ascending order of displeasure are ceremonial slights, expulsion of minor officials, downgrading representatives from ambassador to consul to *chargé d'affairs*, expulsion of an ambassador, ultimatum, and breaking diplomatic relations.

Although not in a negotiating context, there are several interesting examples using clothing as signals. Kemal Ataturk signaled his intention to secularize and westernize Turkey by forcing his people to abandon traditional Islamic garb. Peter the Great did much the same in 17th. century Russia. Ghandi, Khomeini, Qadafi, and Zia all adopted traditional garb to symbolize rejection of western values. Ghandi adopted the spinning wheel as a symbol of national self sufficiency (it remains on the Indian flag). Sun Yat Sen devised the "Mao jacket" to symbolize equality, modernity, and work. Worn by entire Chinese delegations, it conveys remorseless determination.

The characteristics of signals are seen in the subtle series leading to the resumption of diplomatic relations between China and the

United States. When two capsized Americans were rescued by the Chinese, there was none of the usual anti-American propaganda. The United States recognized the signal and allowed American tourists to return from China with $100 in souvenirs. China released the yachtsmen, the U.S. eliminated the ceiling on Chinese souvenirs and China allowed U.S. subsidiaries to sell goods to China. The American table tennis team was invited to China, and U.S. companies were given permission to sell nonstrategic goods to China. Secret negotiations and diplomatic recognition followed.

Less interesting, less subtle, but more common and important are signals based on selection or treatment of envoys. Reagan signaled his desire to improve relations with Greece by appointing a friend of the prime minister as U.S. ambassador. Britain signaled displeasure with martial law in Poland by refusing to receive its new ambassador for weeks. Kennedy refused to invite the French ambassador to the White House to make clear his displeasure with DeGaulle's veto of British admission to the Common Market. Ambassadors can send inappropriately junior diplomats to functions, stay away entirely, or walk out ostentatiously in the middle of someone's speech. Signals are useful precisely because they are flexible, subtle, and disavowable.

Silence

Silence can emphasize a point, give opponents time to absorb a point or reflect on it, or regain the attention of distracted listeners. People are uncomfortable with silence. Failing to respond when expected may lead them to keep talking. They may reveal unintended information or make unplanned concessions. Their discomfort can be increased by jotting something on a piece of paper and staring at it in apparent amazement. Even if opponents do not take the bait, silence can be used to think about what they have just said.

Negotiators answered by silence normally should wait in silence, without retracting, muttering, fidgeting or supplementing what has been said. Alternatives are to ask if opponents understood the proposal, if they need time to discuss it, or would like to take a break. They must make clear nothing new will be said till they get a response to their own statement.

Straw man (Red Herring or Throwaway)

Negotiators sometimes raise issues or take positions in which they have no interest, defend them at length, and finally try to surrender them in exchange for real concessions. Management, desiring a freeze on wages, may say a quarter of the machinists will have to be laid off. A car buyer can start with an unwanted option--expensive

hubcaps, for example. Well into the negotiation the buyer can complain that the price is too steep and give up the hubcaps. At the very
least, this signals real price limits. Skillfully done, it can earn a price
concession greater than the price of the hubcaps. Negotiators must
always assess whether they are faced with straw men or real concerns.

Negotiators faced with straw men often raise their own, then
exchange them for the opponents.' If opponents insist that the straw
men are important, then negotiators can ask for compensation on
other issues that really are important. Negotiators can laugh straw
men off as frivolous, or threaten to deadlock over them, knowing
opponents will not lose a deal to them.

Of course, all this assumes you can identify the straw men correct-
ly. If you do not, they are likely to work as intended. If you mistake
an important issue as a straw man, your counter-tactics could easily
lead to deadlock.

Take it or Leave it

Buyers frequently make clear that a proposal is the last possible
concession (true or not) by saying with at least some emotion ".... and
you can take it or leave it." Negotiators are not without recourse.
Buyers can nibble (see above). Sellers can reply that the balance
could be paid in installments. They can say the offer is acceptable if
the buyer does not require delivery, can accept a delay in filling the
order, will place a large enough order to make such a discount feasi-
ble, or can pay in full in advance. Selecting a condition known from
the exploration phase to be important to the buyer tests just how
"final" the offer is.

Successful or not, this blunt tactic usually weakens the relationship
between the parties. Better than that (see above) is less aggressive.
Still gentler is to respond to an offer by saying it is perfect except for
price, then to suggest a price close to or just below the opponents'
estimated deadlock. Another possibility is to suggest a higher or
lesser quality product or service. This can be made more palatable if
preceded by an explanation that the suggestion best fits the opponents'
own needs.

Threats and Ultimatums

Threats or ultimatums suggest undesirable consequences or penal-
ties if a proposal is not accepted. The ultimatum is the stronger form.
Traditionally, it specifies what the recipient must do, a deadline, and
specific consequences for failure to comply. An ultimatum without a
time limit permits the maker to back off without loss of face, while

preparing to carry it out keeps pressure on opponents. A threat is vaguer than an ultimatum about what the recipient must do, when, or what the consequences will be.

An ultimatum or threat interpreted as hollow or as a bluff, no matter how it was meant, will be ignored and further concessions sought. If seriously intended the recipient may be in for a nasty surprise when negotiations are broken off and the ultimatum or threat is carried out.

Taking a threat seriously even if it is a bluff leaves recipients the choice of accepting the terms or suffering the consequences. Sometimes the threat can be neutralized by transferring the negotiation to higher authority, continuing to negotiate as if the threat never was received, "stopping the clock" until agreement is reached, or bringing in a mediator.

Threats are most effective if made near opponents' deadlines or are coupled with a proposal near their deadlock position. As President Clinton learned, frequent unexecuted threats undermines credibility, noted above as one source of negotiating power. Even this can be exploited. Before attacking Israel in 1972, Sadat carried out a series of bluffs. Preparations for the real attack were seen as just another hollow threat, and the Israelis were surprised. More subtle, Sadat attacked not to defeat Israel, but to create a bargaining climate in which Egypt could negotiate as an equal rather than a vanquished nation (Sadat, 1977). The war made Camp David possible.

Timing

There is a time to speak and a time to listen, a time to question and a time to answer, a time to resist and a time to concede, a time to delay and a time to settle, a time to tell a joke and a time to be serious. A tactic used too early or too late can be as ineffective as making the wrong move entirely. Usually, bluffs are made early and nibbles come late in a negotiation. A hasty response to an offer can make you seem anxious to settle. A long silence may make the opponents anxious. Taking too long to offer a concession may lead opponents to charge you with bad faith bargaining. If you keep talking when opponents are ready to settle, they may deadlock in frustration. A well-timed joke can relieve tension, expose a tactic, or change the pace. A badly-timed (or badly-chosen) one can distract, insult, or belittle. Timing is a subtle skill, developed slowly through experience.

Try to control the pace of a negotiation. Slow things down with aimless banter, endless questions, patient listening, caucuses, changes of personnel, and "stopping the clock." Speed things up with anger, concessions, back channels, best and final offers, linkage, and splitting the difference. Watch for and try to understand opponents' efforts to use timing tactics to *their* advantage.

Four factors affect how much time to spend on preparation. One is the importance of the issues. Dividing the probable savings realized by negotiating by hourly income gives a rough idea of how much time to put into planning a purchase negotiation. Other guidelines can be devised for other situations. Always calculate how much preparation time a negotiation warrants.

Complexity is the second factor determining preparation time. Buying a house requires more preparation than buying a car. Mediating the divorce of a childless couple with no assets requires less preparation than one involving a couple who has operated a successful business together for 20 years, accumulated property and assets, and has children.

The third factor is personnel and expertise. A family buying a car, a lawyer preparing a case, a developer proposing a new resort, and the government preparing to negotiate a multilateral trade treaty illustrate the range.

Finally, deadlines limit preparation. An extreme example is a cruise passenger with a short time in port dealing with a merchant who knows when the ship sails. Negotiators try to delay till they are prepared, or to schedule negotiations when they are strong and opponents are weak. Farm workers do best with contract talks just before harvest; farm owners with talks just after them. When oil prices skyrocketed in 1973, many plastics companies found themselves obligated to buy raw materials at high prices but to deliver products at low prices because their customer and supplier contracts were not synchronized.

Timing is equally important in the bargaining phase. In general, and from most to least desirable from your perspective, opponents might at any time agree to the current proposal, make a concession, make a counteroffer, request more information, caucus, stonewall, take back a concession, make a threat or issue an ultimatum, carry out the ultimatum, or deadlock. Timing can be thought of as trying to increase the likelihood opponents will make choices you prefer. For example, a negotiator sensing the opponent is building up to make a threat might try to head it off with a concession.

Closing becomes technically possible when offers are in the bargaining range of all parties. Negotiators must watch and listen for clues that the time has come to close. Missing them risks deadlock by continuing to bargain with opponents who want to close. The shift from bargaining to closing tactics requires an astute sense of timing.

Toughness

Toughness, negotiating climate, concession-making, and bargaining range are closely intertwined. Negotiating toughness can be quantified as the ratio of Optimistic to Deadlock prices. Divide the former by the latter for sellers and the latter by the former for buyers (inversion avoids comparing whole numbers with fractions).

Negotiators with a small ratio relative to opponents must make smaller or infrequent concessions. Those with a large ratio relative to opponents can make larger or more frequent concessions and still obtain their negotiating objectives. Either approach is legitimate but the two require different tactics. Negotiators should adjust their bargaining range to the concession-making style with which they are most comfortable. In relationships involving repeated negotiations with the same opponent, negotiators should vary both bargaining range and their toughness to avoid becoming predictable.

Knowing one's bargaining range, it is easy to calculate one's own toughness as a guide to appropriate tactics. But, the information necessary to calculate opponents' toughness is unknown. Rather, the formula should be used in reverse to estimate opponents' deadlock position.

Toughness usually pays off, but can make opponents act tough as well, increase the time required to reach agreement, and undermine the bargaining climate. Overdone, it can backfire. Though not in a negotiating context, a classic example of misplaced toughness is giving a bad time to the person checking your luggage onto a plane, which is likely to end up in London if you are going to Hong Kong. Opponents may take revenge through late delivery or late payment, poor quality or frivolous complaints, switching to the competition, or continually changing specifications.

Toughness may stem from media interest--or from efforts to influence opponents through the media. Negotiators find it more difficult to make concessions if their early positions have been publicized, or if they have to appear as fierce defenders of their constituents. Conservatives and business students are most prone to this error.

The opposite of toughness, real or apparent flexibility, can garner concessions from some opponents, particularly those burdened with naive notions of fairness. It can speed a negotiation to a successful conclusion and keep the negotiating climate pleasant. Overdone, for example by offering unreciprocated concessions, it usually leads opponents to conclude that negotiators are so desperate for agreement that listening, patience, and silence will win concessions without giving any. Liberals and therapists are particularly prone to this error.

Venue

Negotiations have taken place on golf courses and in restaurants, restrooms, beds, and every other conceivable setting. A luxury office will awe some opponents but convince others that every deal must cover extravagant overhead costs. The Spartan alternative may impress some opponents with your frugality but convince others you are not doing any business. Somewhere there must be a negotiator who keeps an office of each type and meets opponents in the one most likely to impress them.

Seating arrangements often get considerable attention. Opponents usually sit along opposite sides of a rectangular table, or across a desk from one another, stressing the adversarial nature of the relationship. A round table downplays differences. The famous dispute over table shape for the Vietnamese peace talks really was over whom the parties to the dispute were. North Vietnam insisted the Viet Cong were independent and the South Vietnamese were American puppets. The United States claimed that the Viet Cong were mercenaries fighting for North Vietnam against an independent South Vietnam. A table had to be found that made it clear that there were three sides but left ambiguous who was included on each.

Some negotiators carry such manipulations of temperature, lighting, ventilation, decor, and symbols to extremes. Admiral Rickover's chair was mentioned earlier. During the Korean War truce talks, the Chinese angled lights to shine in the eyes of the UN delegates, placed large Chinese and small UN flags on the table, and sat on the side of the room that, in Asia, was reserved for victors. Other excesses are seating opponents near hot or cold air vents or looking into the glare from the lights or windows. Such bad faith stratagems should be resisted.

Five possible venues are your territory, the opponents' territory, alternating between the two, neutral territory, and negotiations by phone, fax, mail, or e-mail. Home makes efforts to impress opponents possible. It provides quick access to needed staff and information, and control of schedule and atmosphere. Opponents suffer any travel costs and inconveniences. Negotiations can be scheduled to face opponents with remaining in hotels for the weekend unless they agree to your terms. You can prevent or arrange interruptions, and put opponents at ease or not (see bargaining climate, above). Traditionally, negotiations occur in the territory of the stronger party, so negotiating it may put opponents at a psychological disadvantage.

Negotiating on the opponents' territory makes collecting information about them possible, and tactics such as walking out or denying authority easier. Readily agreeing to go to them implies you are so confident you do not need the home field advantage. Arriving early enough to overcome jet lag, keeping return plans flexible, imposing hosting responsibilities, and demanding special facilities can offset home field advantages.

Alternating between territories of opponents is a common compromise. Advantages still are possible. The most common pattern is to hold early rounds on the opponents' territory (to spy) and later ones on your own territory (for psychological advantage). As in all things tactical, blind adherence to the usual may fail. It is better to think about the tactics you wish to use and select the location that best fits each. Opponents may do the same, making venue the subject of preconditions (see above).

Negotiating on neutral territory generally takes place under conditions of low trust, high conflict, or both. Equalizing travel costs, preventing interruption, and denying either side the advantages or disadvantages of negotiating at home may also lead to neutral territory. Even so, you can strive for advantage by handling administrative details such as travel, accommodations, meals, scheduling, and above all, record-keeping. Always keep your own travel arrangements flexible so that opponents cannot put you up against deadline pressure.

Sometimes even agreeing on just what territory is neutral can be difficult. Spain was chosen for the 1991 Israeli-Palestinian negotiations after Algeria and the Netherlands were rejected for being biased toward one side or the other. Norway was chosen for the secret talks that actually resulted in agreement because it provided complete neutrality and confidentiality.

Negotiating by phone reduces travel time and is useful for small or repeated deals. It is a good way to obtain advantage if you are prepared and can catch opponents when they are not. If you are the one caught unawares, make an excuse and return the call when you are prepared. Finally, negotiation by phone is useful if you want to hide your use of reference materials, or to overcome power discrepancies. Newer technologies such as fax and e-mail overcome time differences, eliminate travel, and permit each side to consider or compose documents carefully (see one-text procedure, above).

Weigh the advantages and disadvantages of possible venues, and consider the purposes behind any suggestions made by opponents. The best setting maximizes your control of the bargaining process. It may vary from one phase of the negotiation to another.

A Final Word

There is a tradition in the fiercely competitive diamond industry of sealing every deal with the Yiddish phrase *Mazel brokoff* (Hebrew *baruch*), meaning luck and blessing. In effect, now that the diamond is yours, may it bring you luck so that we will have good dealings in the future. This spirit of competition combined with good will toward opponents is a laudable one to bring to your own negotiations.

Prolegomenon to Negotiation Theory

Benjamin Franklin wrote "Experience is a dear teacher, but fools will learn in no other school (*Poor Richard's Almanack* (1743)." Many negotiators pride themselves on learning by experience. The wise ones also study theory because it incorporates the experience of many, guides not just actions but also analysis and interpretation, and systematically incorporates new knowledge. The better the theory the less costly the mistakes will be. A complete theory strives to describe both process and outcome in predictive form.

Process

The dual-concern model of Pruitt and Carnevale (1993) (Figure 5) and its antecedents [e.g., Blake and Mouton 1964, Carnevale and Pruitt 1992, Killman and Thomas 1978 and Pruitt 1983] provide an excellent starting point for understanding the negotiation process. The dual-concern model asserts that the level of concern for one's own outcomes and the level of concern for one's opponents are independent and important predictors of which of four strategies a negotiator will choose. Some add a fifth strategy, compromise, thought to emerge under conditions of moderate concern for one's own outcomes and moderately high concern for those of opponents' (van de Vliert & Prien 1989).

The dual-concern model has been criticized on several points. Thompson (1990) argues that the model fails to account for win-win solutions that have emerged when opponents have little or no concern with the other party's outcomes, ignores other goals a negotiator may have, and fails to explain why negotiators shift strategy during negotiation. Taken together, these points mean that the dual concern model is not a comprehensive theory of strategic choice.

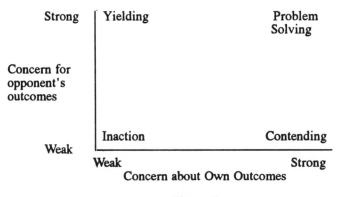

Figure 5
The Dual-Concern Model

In addition, and despite some experimental efforts to do so (re-ported in Pruitt and Carnevale 1993), the independent variables have not been measured directly with sufficient precision to determine how much concern for oneself and for one's opponents is necessary before a negotiator switches strategies. What is needed, then, are proxy variables that are more easily manipulated, measured, and interpreted.

In negotiation, concern for opponents most often stems from long-term relationships or dependency on opponents. It also can stem from special circumstances such as a common identity, a good mood, incentives that give all parties an interest in the success of each individual, and genuine affection toward opponents (Pruitt and Carnevale, 1993). A husband has but one spouse, a child but two parents, a car buyer a choice of many dealers. Of course, some husbands have mistresses, some children have grandparents, and some car buyers may be within practicable distance of only one dealer. Generally, the fewer the number of parties that can satisfy a negotiator's needs, the more cooperative that negotiator is likely to be. Further, it generally is easier to measure than level of concern. Thus, the number of alternative parties with whom negotiation is possible is a likely, measurable proxy for concern for opponents' outcomes.

Turning to the horizontal axis of the dual-concern model, high self-concern can be viewed as stemming from variables such as limited authority, high goals, rigid principles linked to limits and goals, and high accountability to constituents. Thus, it may be desirable to put "resistance to concession" in the place of "concern for one's outcomes" on the horizontal axis of the dual concern model (Pruitt and Carnevale 1993), perhaps measured by somehow combining time between and size of concessions. The amount of risk a person is likely to take also is likely to reflect "concern for one's own outcomes," scaled from -1 to 1. Assume your goal is to double your money. For the purpose of explanation, assume only two equally likely outcomes: reaching your goal (utility = 1) or losing all your money (utility = -1). The overall expected utility is the sum of the utility of all possible outcomes times the likelihood each will occur. With only two possible outcomes, the expected utility is .5*1 + .5*-1 = 0. On the other hand, if no investment is made, your money will remain intact, with no chance of doubling or losing it (utility = 0). In this situation, a risk accepting negotiator would agree, a risk averse negotiator would deadlock, and a risk neutral investor would be indifferent among the choices (de Mesquita, 1981).

Combining these ideas leads to Figure 6. The axes and strategies they predict have been renamed. Renaming the axes incorporates the ideas discussed above. Renaming the strategies gives them parallel grammatical form and makes them easier to remember.

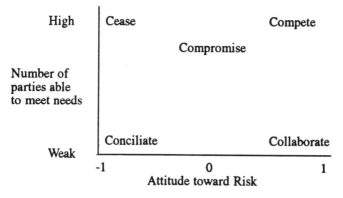

Figure 6
Five Basic Negotiating Strategies

The dual concern model predicts that a negotiator for whom self-concern is paramount will employ competitive tactics. If the tactics are unsuccessful, agreement is possible only if the negotiator changes to collaborative tactics (Pruitt and Carnevale 1993). This is as close as the dual concern model comes to taking account of the opponent, because it has been developed assuming both sides will have the same level of concern on both dimensions. In fact, opponents may not have the same attitude toward risk or the same number of alternative parties with whom they can reach agreement. Rather, they too will have a negotiating strategy predicted by their attitude toward risk and the number of parties with whom they can reach agreement. Figure 7 extends the dual-concern model to a strategic interaction model that predicts the consequences in a two-party negotiation.

"L" [Lose] refers to a competitive strategy in which concessions tend to be small, infrequent, and often made primarily to keep the other party from ceasing negotiations. "W" [Win] refers to a collaborating strategy in which the negotiator tries to learn and meet the needs of the opponent while communicating the legitimacy of his own needs to the opponent. Thus, for example, "W-W" indicates the *only* conditions in which both parties are likely to pursue collaborative or win-win negotiations. The frequencies in the chart may explain why win-win negotiations seem more common in the classroom than in the real world! "U" [Unstable] indicates cells in which at least one negotiator is likely to change over time to one of the other four strategies (addressing the criticism of the dual-concern model that it does not explain such strategic switches). "D" refers to Deadlock, in which case the strategy and outcome are synonymous. The combinations were reached by speculation and discussion. Thus, the reader may arrive at quite different conclusions for particular cells, which should foster debate.

	Concil-iate	Collab-orate	Compro-mise	Cease	Compete
Conciliate	L-L	L-W	L-W	L-W	L-W
Collaborate	W-L	W-W	W-L	L-W	U
Compromise	W-L	L-W	W-L	L-W	L-W
Cease	W-L	W-L	W-L	D	D
Compete	W-L	U	W-L	D	W-L

Figure 7
Strategic Interaction Model

Strategy Shifts

Negotiators may change strategy during a negotiation. Pruitt and Carnevale (1993) emphasize changes toward more innovative and cooperative outcomes, but this need not be the case. Nor are changes necessarily in the same direction or at the same rate for both parties. Thus, the "Strategic Interaction Model" is useful in understanding the tactics employed at any particular point in the negotiating process, how these strategies interact, and how they *might* change over the course of a negotiation. Further, it provides a model for interpreting the tactics of opponents and a guide to selecting tactics to influence the direction the negotiations are taking and to achieving the outcome desired.

Outcome

Rational negotiators will not agree unless the highest price one party will pay exceeds the lowest price the other party will accept.

When this is the case, a "settlement range" is said to exist. Negotiating power, the ability to influence others' decisions, may be the single best predictor of where within the settlement range agreement will be reached.

Goldman (1991) provides a starting point for measuring negotiating power, portraying factors that strengthen or weaken a negotiator on either side of an old fashion balance. An alternative formulation incorporates six measurable factors affecting negotiating power:

V Value of an offer to opponents, estimated in $, which strengthens the offeror. The probability that the estimate is correct is p.

B Best alternative to agreement [Fisher and Ury's BATNA], in $. The closer V gets to B the stronger the offeror gets.

C Cost (past and future) to the offeror of negotiation, in $. Given equal resources, the higher cost negotiator has less power.

D Deadline for reaching agreement in years.

E Experience as a negotiator in years. All else being equal, the more experienced negotiator has more power

R Ranked priority of the issue (i) to opponent. The higher the rank, the more power it gives the offeror.

Using subscripts a and b to distinguish one negotiator from the other, and considering whether a factor strengthens or weakens a negotiator, the negotiating power (P) of negotiator "a" on a single issue can be hypothesized as:

$$P_a = (D_a/D_b * E_a/E_b)(B_b - C_a + C_b + p_b * V_b)$$

Recognizing that power may vary from one issue to another, it must be summed across all issues:

$$P_a = \sum_{i=1}^{n} P_a (D_a/D_b * E_a/E_b)(B_b - C_a + C_b + p_b V_b)$$

The power of negotiator "b" is the same formula with the subscripts reversed:

$$P_b = \sum_{i=1}^{n} P_b (D_b/D_a * E_b/E_a)(B_a - C_b + C_a + p_a * V_a)$$

Finally, relative Power can be expressed as a ratio

$$P_a : P_b$$

that predicts where within the settlement range agreement will be reached. These formulas are conceptual and speculative but make empirical testing possible, as each can be operationalized and manipulated. For example, the portion of the formula that states:

$$(D_a/D_b * E_a/E_b)$$

implies that a negotiator long on experience faced with a short deadline may not be at a significant disadvantage against an opponent with a distant deadline, if the opponent is sufficiently inexperienced.

The remaining question, suggested by Fraser and Hipel (1984), is whether parties will adhere to an agreement, or in their terminology, will prove "stable." They think of proposals as options that may be included (indicated by a 1) or not (indicated by a 0) in the final agreement. If there are two negotiators, each advocating two options, there are sixteen possible agreements (2^4), each represented by a column of 1's and 0's to indicate inclusion or exclusion:

```
Negotiator 1 Option A:  0 1 0 1 0 1 0 1 0 1 0 1 0 1 0 1
Negotiator 1 Option B:  0 0 1 1 0 0 1 1 0 0 1 1 0 0 1 1
Negotiator 2 Option C:  0 0 0 0 1 1 1 1 0 0 0 0 1 1 1 1
Negotiator 2 Option D:  0 0 0 0 0 0 0 0 1 1 1 1 1 1 1 1
```

One of the possibilities, represented by the column of 0's, is deadlock. One of the possibilities, represented by the column of 1's, is agreement to all four proposals. It is possible that some of the possibilities are contradictory. For example, if Option A represents "no down payment" and Option C represents "a substantial down payment," columns 6, 7, 14 and 16 are impossible agreements and can be eliminated from further consideration. Once they have been eliminated, the columns can be reordered from left to right to indicate each negotiator's ranking of each possible agreement, forming a "preference vector." For example, if Negotiator 1 ranked the issues A, B. D, but would deadlock before accepting any agreement including C, Negotiator 1's preference vector might be:

```
Negotiator 1 Option A:  1 1 1 1 0 0 0 0 1 1 1 0 1 0 0 0
Negotiator 1 Option B:  0 1 1 0 1 1 0 0 0 1 1 1 0 1 0 0
Negotiator 2 Option C:  0 0 0 0 0 0 0 0 1 1 1 1 1 1 1 1
Negotiator 2 Option D:  0 0 1 1 0 1 1 0 1 1 0 1 0 0 0 1
```

Presumably, Negotiator 2 would rank the issues differently.

With preference vectors specified and ordered for all parties, they can be analyzed mathematically to identify which agreements are likely to be adhered to if accepted by both negotiators (Fraser and Hipel, 1984). Fraser and Hipel also provide means of analyzing preference vectors when the other negotiators are misunderstood (perhaps because they are lying), incomplete (because not all options or parties are known), or in which parties form coalitions.

Process and Outcome Combined

Preference vectors predict which options will be included in the final settlement. Relative power predicts where agreement will be reached within the settlement range (so provides a means of estimating what it is). The joint strategies pursued will determine both the relationship among the parties and the extent to which the Pareto Optimal Frontier is reached. That is, we must reconsider Figure 6 taking account of power and preferences if we are to predict outcomes in all possible negotiating situations. The possibilities are discussed in turn below, following the convention of assigning a two-digit number to each cell representing the row first and the column second. Again, the suggestions are speculative rather than empirical. A few, however, are justified by the literature. For example, a number of studies (Bazerman *et. al.* 1985, Carneval & Lawler 1986, Neale & Bazerman 1985, Humber & Neale 1986) have concluded that when both parties are motivated by self-interest, Pareto optimization is unlikely unless they also are motivated by concern for the opponent.

11   Both parties have more important things to worry about including maintaining good relations with one another. This suggests both will quickly drop to and settle at their BATNA.

12 or 21   The collaborator is likely to suggest creative ideas that improve on both BATNA's but when the distribution is made the conciliator is more likely to get the larger concessions. The solution is likely to be lose-win, is unlikely to be Pareto optimal, but is likely to be nearer to it than will occur in cell 13.

13 or 31   The conciliator is unlikely to push the compromiser, who is likely to make most of the proposals, and thus to get the better part of the deal. The most likely outcome is an affable, non-optimal, uncreative agreement reached by haggling separately on each issue.

14 or 41   The conciliators are most likely to offer concessions until reaching their BATNA just to keep the party that wants to cease negotiations at the table. That party may make demands but is unlikely to put any energy into creative proposals.

15 or 51   The result is unlikely to be much different than in cell 14,

with the competitors getting the lion's share and the conciliators forced down to their BATNA. However, the negotiating climate and the process will be much different, with the competing negotiators taking the lead in pushing for concessions, rather than the conciliators offering them.

22   This cell represents the idealized Win-Win negotiation of the textbooks. Both sides will emphasize their common interests, and they will work together to meet the needs of all parties. Factors such as creativity, knowledge, and time will determine whether the Pareto Optimal Frontier is reached, and objective criteria set by the negotiators rather than power will determine the distribution.

23 or 32   The likely result is a near Pareto optimal solution slightly favoring the collaborators, who have little incentive to try to convert opponents into collaborators.

24 or 42   The most likely result is a Win-Lose solution favoring the party that prefers cessation of negotiations to putting much effort into them, for much the same reasons as in cell 14. This likelihood provides the collaborators with an incentive to try to convert their opponents into collaborators or at least into compromisers. The odds of success are low.

25 or 52   The most likely result is that one party will convert the other to their own style of negotiating! If the collaborator succeeds, the situation becomes indistinguishable from cell 22. If the competitor succeeds, the situation becomes indistinguishable from cell 55.

33   This cell represents negotiations reduced to simple haggling, likely to result in the parties splitting the difference issue by issue.

34 or 43   The compromisers will have to make concessions to keep the party that wants to cease negotiations at the table. Presumably they will be less willing to do so than conciliators or collaborators, so that agreement will take longer if negotiations are continued at all.

35 or 53   Presumably the competitor will make small concessions at a slow rate if at all, and will drive the compromisers to or near to their BATNA.

44   With neither the substance nor the relationship important to either party, the most likely result is a fairly quick, probably polite

45 or 54   With neither substance nor the relationship important to the party that wants to cease negotiations, the tactics of the competitive negotiator are likely to result in a quick deadlock.

55   If both parties are competitive, the result *could* be the bruising kind of Win-Lose negotiation described by writers such as Fisher and Ury (1981). That is, each side is determined not to get taken, and relies on pressure, intimidation, and abuse to get as much as possible from the other side. However, if as is likely both competitors are rational, they are more likely to persist in searching for tradeoffs that will leave both parties better off. This explains why competitive negotiators can and often do reach Pareto Optimal solutions.

Conclusion

Theory building in any discipline is a complex process of fact-gathering, interpretation, and synthesis. Theorists from many disciplines have contributed to understanding particular aspects of negotiation. This chapter attempts to integrate the work of some of them into a more comprehensive description of both the process and the outcome of negotiations. It asserts that five variables are sufficient to predict how two negotiators will interact and what the outcome will be. It suggests how the five variables can be operationalized. It is intended, as theory should, to suggest experimentation, synthesis, and debate.

Works Mentioned in the Text

Axtell, R. (1993). *Do's and Taboos Around the World.* New York: John Wiley & Sons, Inc.

Bazerman M. *et. al.* (1985). Integrative bargaining in a competitive market. *Organizational Behavior of Human Decision Processes, 35*: 294-313.

Black's Law Dictionary (1968). St. Paul, MN: West Publishing

Blake R. and Mouton, J. (1964). *The Managerial Grid.* Houston: Gulf.

Brooks, W. (Spring 1994). Negotiating with an adversary, *IGCC Newsletter.* San Diego: University of California.

Bullfinch, T. (1970). *Mythology.* New York: Thomas Y. Crowell.

Carneval, P. and Lawler, E. (1986). Time pressure and the development of integrative agreement in bilateral negotiation. *Journal of Conflict Resolution 30*: 636-59.

Carnevale P. and Pruitt, D. (1992). Negotiation and mediation. *Annual Review of Psychology 43*, 531-582

de Mesquita, B. (1981). *The War Trap.* New Haven: Yale University Press.

el-Sadat, A. (1977). *In Search of Identity.* New York: Harper & Row.

Fischer, D. (1970). *Historians' Fallacies*. New York: Harper Torchbooks.

Fisher, R. and W. Ury (1981). *Getting to ̲2s: Negotiating Agreement Without Giving In*. Boston: Hougton Mifflin.

Fraser, N. and Hipel, K. (1984). *Conflict Analysis: Models and Resolutions*. New York: North-Holland.

Goldman, A. (1991). *Settling for More: Mastering Negotiating Strategies and Techniques*. Washington, DC: BNA Books.

Huber, V. and Neale, M. (1986). Effects of cognitive heuristics and goals on negotiator performance and subsequent goal setting. *Organizational Behavior of Human Decision Processes, 38*: 342-65.

Ikle, F. (1964). *How Nations Negotiate*. Millwood, NY: Krauss.

Joy, C. (1970). *How Communists Negotiate*. Santa Monica, CA: Fidelis Publishers, Inc.

Katzer, J. *et. al.* (1982). *Evaluating Information*. Reading, MA: Addison-Wesley Publishing Company.

Killmann, R. and Thomas, K. (January 1978). Four perspectives on conflict management: an attributional framework for organizing descriptive and normative theory. *Academy of Management Review 3, 1*.

Kriesberg, L., *et. al.* eds, (1989). *Intractable Conflicts and Their Transformation*. Syracuse NY: Syracuse University Press.

Lax, D. & Sebenius, J. (1986). *The Manager as Negotiator*. New York: The Free Press

Neale, M. and Bazerman, M. (1985). The effects of framing and negotiator overconfidence on bargaining behaviors and outcomes. *Academy of Management Journal 28*: 34-49.

Pakenham, T. (1979). *The Boer War*. New York: Random House.

Pruitt, D. (November/December 1983). Strategic choice in negotiation. *American Behavioral Scientist, 27, 2*.

Pruitt, D. and Carnevale, P. (1993). *Negotiation in Social Conflict*. Pacific Grove, CA: Brooks/Cole

Pruitt, D. and Rubin, J. (1986). *Social Conflict: Escalation, Stalemate, and Settlement*. New York: McGraw-Hill

Raiffa, H. (1982). *Art and Science of Negotiation*. Cambridge, MA: Harvard University Press.

Romer, J. (1984). *Ancient Lives*. New York: Holt, Rinehart and Winston.

Rubin, J. *et. al*. (1994) *Social Conflict: Escalation, Stalemate, and Settlement* (2nd ed). New York: McGraw-Hill.

Shirer, W. (1959). *Rise and Fall of the Third Reich*. New York: Simon and Schuster, Inc.

Thompson, L. (1990). Negotiation behavior and outcomes: empirical evidence and theoretical issues. *Psychology Bulletin 108*: 515-32.

van de Vliert, E., (1990). Positive effects of Conflict: A Field Assessment. *The International Journal of Conflict Management, 1*.

van de Vliert, E. and Prein, H., (1989). The difference in the meaning of forcing in the conflict management of actors and observers. In Rahim, M. A. ed. *Managing Conflict: An Interdisciplinary Approach*. New York: Praeger.

Wilson, J. (1951). *The Burden of Egypt*. Chicago: University of Chicago Press.

Bibliography

Kelly Kartchner and Randy Hatago

Anyone who has attempted to classify books into a useful number of categories will understand that arbitrary decisions must be made. Should a book on negotiating real estate covering both rental and residential properties be listed under business negotiations, personal negotiations, or both? Listing books in every category in which they fit would unnecessarily lengthen the bibliography.

Instead, this bibliography assigns each book to a single category. Readers searching for books on consumer, divorce, ethnic, family, legal, neighborhood and similar disputes will find them in the category "Community and Individual Conflict." Those interested in areas such as purchasing (business, government, or personal), salary negotiations, labor, and interdepartmental disputes will find them in "Organizational Conflict." Those concerned with facility siting, development, public policy, natural resource and related disputes will find the most useful material under "Environmental Conflict." Those interested in international business, diplomacy, intercultural communication, hostage negotiations, and war should turn to the section on "International Conflict." There also are separate sections for "Fiction" that emphasizes negotiations, for "General and Theoretical" works, and a list of "Journals" that specialize in, or have frequent articles on negotiations and conflict management.

Where an author has written a series of similar books, or has published a subsequent edition, only the most recent one is listed.

This bibliography concentrates on the period 1985-1994. It includes a few older entries, either because they are the most recent to address a topic or they have some special interest. Bibliographies, like the latest computers, are out-of-date as soon as they are available. This one was updated in 1994.

Community and Individual Conflict

Academy of Family Mediators (n.d.). *Standards of Practice for Family and Divorce Mediation.* Portland, OR: Author.

Ahron, C. and Rogers R. (1987). *Divorced Families: A Multidisciplinary Development View.* New York: Norton.

American Arbitration Association (1986). *Commercial Dispute Resolution: A Resource Guide.* New York: Author.

American Bar Association (1989). *Alternative Means of Family Dispute Resolutions.* Washington, DC: Author.

Annechino, D. (1993). *How to Buy the Most Car for the Least Money.* New York: Signet.

Bragg, W. (1993). *In the Driver's Seat: the New Car Buyer's Negotiating Bible.* New York: Random House.

Bucher, B. (1987). *Winning Them Over: How to Negotiate Successfully with your Kids.* New York: Times Books.

Cahn, D. (1992). *Conflict in Intimate Relationships.* New York: Guilford Press.

Center for Law and Social Policy (1988). *Public Benefits Issues in Divorce Cases: A Manual for Mediators.* Washington, DC: NIDR.

Chalmers, W. (1974). *Racial Negotiations: Potentials and Limitations.* Ann Arbor: University of Michigan.

Coolidge, G. *et. al.* (1989). *Women Negotiate.* Boston, MA: Simmons College Graduate School of Management.

Craver, C. (1993). *Effective Legal Negotiation and Settlement.* Charlottesville, VA: Michie Co.

Creighton, J. (1991). *Don't Go Away Mad: How to Make Peace With Your Partner.* New York: Doubleday.

Croom, D. (1989). *Dispute Resolution and the Courts: An Annotated Bibliography.* Washington, DC: NIDR.

Crowley, T. (1994). *Settle it Out of Court: How to Resolve Business and Personal Disputes Using Mediation, Arbitration, and Negotiation.* New York: J. Wiley.

Davis, G. (1992). *Making Amends: Mediation and Reparation in Criminal Justice.* London: Routledge.

Diane Publishing Company (1993). *S.W.A.T. and Hostage Negotiation.* Upland, CA: Author

Doane, G. (n.d.) *Hostage Negotiator's Manual.* San Rafael, CA: Police Press.

Dolan, J. (1992). *Negotiate Like the Pros.* New York, NY: Perigee Books.

Donohue, W. (1991). *Communication, Marital Dispute, and Divorce Mediation.* Hillsdale, NJ: Lawrence Erlbaum Associates.

Donohue, W. (1992). *Managing Interpersonal Conflict.* Newbury Park: Sage Publications.

Doyle, S., and Haydock, R. (1991). *Without the Punches: Resolving Disputes without Litigation.* Minneapolis, MN: Equilaw.

Duffy, K. et. al. (1991). *Community Mediation: a Handbook for Practitioners and Researchers.* New York: Guilford Press.

Edelman, J. and Crain, M. (1993). *The Tao of Negotiation.* New York: Harper Business.

Emerick-Cayton, T. (1993). *Divorcing with Dignity: Mediation, the Sensible Alternative.* Louisville, KY: Westminster/John Knox Press.

Erickson, S. and Erickson, M. (1988). *Family Mediation Casebook, Theory and Process.* New York: Brunner/Mazell.

Federal Trade Commission (1991). *Road to Resolution: Settling Consumer Disputes.* Washington, DC: NIDR.

Folberg, J. and Claus, K. (1989). *Dispute Resolution Education and Training: A Video Reference Guide.* Washington, DC NIDR.

Folberg, J. and Milne, A. (1988). *Divorce Mediation: Theory and Practice.* New York: Guilford Press.

Gifford, D. (1989). *Legal Negotiation: Theory and Applications.* St. Paul, MN: West Publishing.

Halpern, R. (1991). *Plantiff's Personal Injury Negotiation Strategies.* New York: Wiley Law Publications.

Hawkins, L. et. al. (1992). *The Legal Negotiator: a Handbook for Managing Legal Negotiations more Effectively.* Melbourne, Australia: Longman Professional.

Haynes, J. (1989). *Mediating Divorce : Casebook of Strategies for Successful Family Negotiations.* San Francisco: Jossey-Bass.

Haynes, J. (1994). *The Fundamentals of Family Mediation.* Albany: State University of New York Press.

Hofrichter, R. (1987). *Neighborhood Justice in Capitalistic Society* Westpoint, CT: Greenwood Press.

Hopley, R. (1989). *Strategic Management in the Public Arena.* Washington, DC: National Institute for Dispute Resolution.

Ingleby, R. (1988). *Mediation and the Legal Process.* Oxford: Oxford University Press.

Keltner, J. (1987). *Mediation: Toward a Civilized System of Dispute Resolution.* Annandale, VA: SCA.

Kershen, H. and Meirowitz, C. (1992). *Strategies for Impasse Resolution.* Amityville, N.Y.: Baywood.

Krebel, F. and Clay, G. (1989). *Before You Sue: How to Get Justice Without Going to Court.* New York: William Morrow and Co.

Kressel, K., et. al. (1989). *Mediation Research: The Process and Effectiveness of Third Party Intervention.* San Francisco: Jossey-Bass.

Kritzer, H. (1991). *Let's Make a Deal: Understanding the Negotiation Process in Ordinary Litigation.* Madison: University of Wisconsin.

Kritzer, H. (1992). *Toward a Theory of Representation in Adversary Proceedings.* Madison, WI: Institute for Legal Studies, University of Wisconsin-Madison Law School.

Lassar, T. (1990). *City Deal Making.* Washington DC: ULI-the Urban Land Institute.

Lisnek, P. (1992). *A Lawyer's Guide to Effective Negotiation and Mediation.* St. Paul, MN: West Pub. Co.

Lovenheim, P. (1989). *Mediate, Don't Litigate.* New York: McGraw-Hill.

Lynch, E. (1992). *Negotiation and Settlement*. Rochester, NY: Lawyers Cooperative.

MacWilson, A. (1992). *Hostage-Taking Terrorism: Incident-Response Strategy*. New York: St. Martin's Press.

Maynard, D. (1985). *Inside Plea Bargaining: The Language of Negotiation*. New York: Plenum.

Messmer, H., and Otto, H. (1992). *Restorative Justice on Trial: Pitfalls and Potentials of Victim-Offender Mediation: International Research Perspectives*. Boston: Kluwer Academic Publishers.

Mitchell, R. (1990). *The Mediator Handbook*. Columbus, OH: Center for Dispute Resolution, Capital University Law and Graduate Center.

Moore, C. (1986). *The Mediation Process*. San Francisco: Jossey Bass.

Muhlstein, E. (1990). *A Guide to Facilitating Social Problem Solving with Children Ages Two through Five*. Pasadena: Pacific Oaks, CA.

NIDR (1988). *Dispute Resolution and the Courts*. Washington, DC: Author.

Paulson, B. and Sander, F. (1987). *Alternative Dispute Resolution: An ADR Primer*. Washington, DC: American Bar Association

Piper, C. (1993). *The Responsible Parent: a Study of Divorce Mediation*. London: Harvester Wheatsheaf.

Prutzman, D. *et. al.* (1988). *The Friendly Classroom for a Small Planet*. Nyack, NY: Childrens' Creative Response to Conflict Project.

Saposnek, D. (1987). *Mediating Child Custody Disputes*. San Francisco: Jossey Bass.

Shailor, J. (1994). *Empowerment in Dispute Mediation: a Critical Analysis of Communication*. Westport, Conn.: Praeger.

Thibaut, J. and Walker, L. (1976). *Procedural Justice: A Psychological Analysis*. New York: Wiley.

Thompson, L. (1986). *The Rescuers: The World's Top Anti-Terrorist Units*. Boulder, CO: Paladin

White, J. (1976). *The Lawyer as Negotiator*. West Publishing, MN

Williams, R. (1977). *Mutual Accommodation: Ethnic Conflict and Cooperation*. Minneapolis: University of Minnesota Press.

Environmental Conflict

Amy, D. (1987). *The Politics of Environmental Mediation*. New York: Columbia University.

Bacow, L. and Wheeler, M. (1985). *Environmental Dispute Resolution*. New York: Plenum.

Barrett, S. (1992). *Convention on Climate Change: Economic Aspects of Negotiations*. Paris: Organisation for Economic Co-operation and Development.

Bingham, G. (1988). *Resolving Environmental Disputes*. Washington, DC: Conservation Foundation.

Blackford, C. (1992). *A Review of Environmental Mediation: Theory and Practice*. Lincoln, New Zealand: Centre for Resource Management, Lincoln University.

Brion, D. (1991). *Essential Industry and the NIMBY Phenomenon*. New York: Quorum

Burton, J. (1987). *Resolving Deep-rooted Conflict: A Handbook*. Lanham, MD: University Press of America.

Carpenter, S. and Kennedy, W. (1988). *Managing Public Disputes: A Practical Guide to Handling Conflict and Reaching Agreements*. San Francisco: Jossey-Bass.

Carroll, J. (1988). *International Environmental Diplomacy: The Management and Resolution of Transfrontier Environmental Problems*. Cambridge: Cambridge University.

Crowfoot, J. E., and Wondolleck, J. (1990). *Environmental Disputes: Community Involvement in Conflict Resolution*. Washington, D.C.: Island Press.

Duffy, K. *et al.* (1991). *Community Mediation: A Handbook for Practioners and Researchers*. New York: The Guilford Press.

Faure, G., and Rubin, J. (1993). *Culture and Negotiation: the Resolution of Water Disputes*. Newbury Park, CA: SAGE Publications.

Frumkin, H. (1991). *Crisis at our Doorstep: Occupational and Environmental Health Implications for Mexico-U.S.-Canada Trade Negotiations.* Chicago, Illinois: National Safe Workplace Institute.

Gamman, J. (1994). *Overcoming Obstacles in Environmental Policymaking: Creating Partnerships through Mediation.* Albany: State University of New York Press.

Gorczynski, D. (1991). *Insiders Guide to Environmental Negotiation.* New York: Lewis Publishers.

Madigan, D. *et al.* (1990). *New Approaches to Resolving Local Public Disputes.* Washington, DC: National Institute for Dispute Resolution

Netter, E. (1992). *Negotiating and Mediating Land Use Disputes.* Chicago, IL: American Institute of Certified Planners.

O'Hare, M., *et. al.* (1983). *Facility Siting and Public Opposition.* Van Nostrand.

Oregon Department of Land Conservation and Development (1989). *Dispute Resolution: A Handbook for Land Use Planners and Resource Managers.* Salem, OR: Author.

Paine, R. (1982). *Dam a River, Dam a People?: Saami Livelihood and the Al Ta/Kautokeino Hydro-Electric Project.* Cambridge, MA: Cultural Survival.

Parson, E. and Zeckhauser, R. (1993). *Equal Measures and Fair Burdens: Negotiating Environmental Treaties in an Unequal World.* Cambridge, MA: Center for Science and International Affairs, John F. Kennedy School of Government, Harvard University.

Pritzker, D. and Dalton, D. (1990). *Negotiated Rulemaking Sourcebook.* Washington, DC: Office of the Chairman.

Rabe, B. (1989). *The Politics of Environmental Dispute Resolution.* Ann Arbor: CRSO, Center for Research on Social Organization, University of Michigan.

Rodman, K. (1988). *Sanctity Versus Sovereignty: United States and the Nationalization of Natural Resource Investments.* New York: Columbia University.

Sheldon, H. and Claydon, J. (1991). *Negotiations in Planning: Local Authority/Developer Negotiations.* Bristol: Bristol Polytechnic, Dept. of Town and Country Planning.

Sjostedt, G. (1993). *International Environmental Negotiation.* Newbury Park, Calif: Sage Publications.

Sullivan, T. (1985). *Resolving Development Disputes Through Negotiations.* New York: Plenum.

Susskind, L. *et. al.* (1992). *International Environmental Treaty Making* Cambridge: Harvard Law School

Susskind, L. *et. al.* (1990). *Nine Case Studies in International Environmental Negotiation.* Cambridge, Mass.: Harvard Law School.

Susskind, L. (1993). *Environmental Diplomacy: Negotiating more Effective Global Agreements.* New York: Oxford University Press.

Susskind, L. and Cruikshank, J. (1987). *Breaking the Impasse: Consensual Approaches to Resolving Public Disputes.* New York: Basic Books.

Susskind, L. *et. al.* (1984). *Resolving Environmental Regulatory Disputes.* Cambridge, MA: Schenkman.

Taylor, T. (1989). *A Practical Theory of Negotiation for Planners.* Washington, DC: NIDR, National Institute for Dispute Resolution.

Teply, L. (1992). *Legal Negotiation in a Nutshell.* St. Paul, MN: West Pub. Co.

Trolldalen, J. (1992). *International Environmental Conflict Resolution: The Role of the United Nations.* Washington, D.C.: NIDR.

Wondolleck, J. (1988). *Public Lands Conflict and Resolution.* New York: Plenum.

Fiction

Aron, R. (1962). *Paix et guerre entre les nations.* Paris: Calman-Levy.

Forsyth, F. (1989). *The Negotiator.* New York: Bantam.

Francis, D. (1984). *The Danger.* New York: Fawcett Crest.

Martin, M. (1978). *The Final Conclave.* New York: Stein and Day.

Tolkin, M. (1992). *The Player: a Novel.* New York: Vintage.

Walder, F. (1959). *The Negotiators.* McDowell, Obolensky.

General and Theory

Anastasi, T. (1993). *Personality Negotiating: Conflict Without Casualty.* New York: Sterling Pub. Co.

Anderson, K. (1994). *Getting What You Want: How to Reach Agreement and Resolve Conflicts Every Time.* New York, NY: Plume.

Arrow, K. (1993). *Information Acquisition and the Resolution of Conflict.* Stanford, CA: Stanford Center on Conflict and Negotiation, Stanford University.

Bartos, O. (1974). *Process and Outcomes of Negotiations.* New York: Columbia University Press.

Bazerman, M. and Neale, M. (1992). *Negotiating Rationally.* New York: Maxwell Macmillan International.

Bermant, G., *et. al.* (1978). *The Ethics of Social Intervention.* Washington, Hemisphere.

Brams, S. (1990). *Negotiation Games: Applying Game Theory to Bargaining and Arbitration.* New York: Routledge.

Breslin, J. and Rubin, J. (1993). *Negotiation Theory and Practice.* Cambridge, MA.: Program on Negotiation at Harvard Law School.

Buntzman, G. (1989). *Managing Conflict: An Interdisciplinary Approach.* New York: Prager.

Burton, J., ed (1990). *Conflict: Human Needs Theory:* New York: St. Martin's.

Caillaud, B., and Hermalin, B. (1991). *The Use of an Agent in a Signalling Model.* Berkeley, CA: University of California.

Christopher, E. and Smith, L. (1991). *Negotiation Training through Gaming: Strategies, Tactics, and Manoeuvres.* London: Nichols/GP Pub.

Cialdini, R. (1988). *Influence: Science and Practice.* New York: Scott Foresman.

Cross, J. (1969). *The Economics of Bargaining.* New York: Basic Books.

Davis, G. and Roberts, M. (1988). *Access to Agreement.* New York: Open University Press.

Dekel, E. (1989). *Simultaneous Offers and the Inefficiency of Bargaining: A Two-Period Example.* Berkeley, CA: University of California.

Fisher, R. and Brown, S. (1988). *Getting Together: Building a Relationship that Gets To Yes.* Boston: Houghton Mifflin.

Fisher, R. and Ury, W. (1981). *Getting to Yes: Negotiating Agreement Without Giving In.* Boston: Hougton Mifflin.

Fisher, R. *et. al.* (1994). *Beyond Machiavelli.* Cambridge, MA: Harvard

Folger, J. and Jones, T. (1994). *New Directions in Mediation: Communication Research and Perspectives.* Newbury Park: Sage.

Fowler, A. (1990). *Negotiations: Skills and Strategies.* London: Institute of Personnel Management.

Fraser, N. and Hipel, K. (1984). *Conflict Analysis: Models and Resolutions.* New York: North-Holland.

Freund, J. (1992). *Smart Negotiating: How to Make Good Deals in the Real World.* New York: Simon and Schuster.

Fried, C. (1978). *Right and Wrong.* Cambridge MA: Harvard University Press.

Fuller, G. (1991). *The Negotiator's Handbook.* Englewood Cliffs, NJ: Prentice Hall.

Galanter, M. (1991). *The Transformation of American Business Disputing?: Some Preliminary Observations.* Madison, WI: Institute for Legal Studies, University of Wisconsin.

Gilson, R. (1993). *Cooperation and Competition in Litigation.* Stanford, CA: Stanford Center on Conflict and Negotiation, Stanford University.

Goldberg, S., *et. al.* (1985). *Dispute Resolution.* Boston: Little Brown and Co.

Goldman, A. (1991). *Settling for More: Mastering Negotiating Strategies and Techniques.* Washington, DC: BNA Books.

Gottlieb, M., and Healy, W. (1990). *Making Deals: the Business of Negotiating.* New York: Institute of Finance.

Gray, B. (1988). *Collaborating*. San Francisco: Jossey-Bass.

Hall, L. (1993). *Negotiation Strategies for Mutual Gain: the Basic Seminar of the Harvard Program on Negotiation*. Newbury Park: Sage.

Halpern, A. (1992). *Negotiating Skills*. London: Blackstone Press.

Hoffman, B. (1990). *Conflict, Power, and Persuasion: Negotiating Effectively*. North York, CANADA: Captus Press.

Hylton, K. (1993). *An Economic Theory of Bargaining Obligations*. Chicago, IL: University of Chicago Law School.

Ilich, J. (1992). *Dealbreakers and Breakthroughs: the Ten Most Common and Costly Negotiation Mistakes and How to Overcome Them*. New York: Wiley.

Johnson, R. (1993). *Negotiation Basics: Concepts, Skills, and Exercises*. Newbury Park, CA: Sage Publications.

Kahneman, D. (1993). *Conflict Resolution*. Stanford, CA: Stanford Center on Conflict and Negotiation, Stanford University.

Karrass, C. (1992). *The Negotiating Game: How to Get What You Want*. New York: Harper Business.

Karrass, C. (1993). *Give and Take: the Complete Guide to Negotiating Strategies and Tactics*. New York: Harper Business.

Katz, M. (1991). *Game-Playing Agents: Unobservable Contracts as Precommitments*. Berkeley, CA: University of California.

Keltner, D. (1993). *Assumed Differences and Hidden Similarities*. Stanford, CA: Stanford Center on Conflict and Negotiation, Stanford University.

Kemper, R. (1994). *Negotiation Literature: a Bibliographic Essay*. Metuchen, NJ: Scarecrow Press.

Kim, S. (1991). *Conflict, Negotiation and Dispute Resolution*. Cambridge, MA: Program on Negotiation at Harvard Law School.

Kniveton, B. (1989). *The Psychology of Bargaining*. Brookfield, VA: Avebury.

82 *Negotiation Tactics*

Kolb, D. (1992). *Is it Her Voice or Her Place that Makes a Difference? A Consideration of Gender Issues in Negotiation.* Kingston, canada: Industrial Relations Centre, Queen's University.

Koren, L. and Goodman, P. (1991). *The Haggler's Handbook.* New York: W. W. Norton and Company.

Kuhn, R. (1988). *Dealmaker: All the Negotiating Skills and Secrets you Need.* New York: Wiley.

Kumar, R. (1989). *Affect, Cognition and Decision Making in Negotiation: an Analysis of American and Japanese Business Negotiations.* Unpublished doctoral dissertation.

Kuon, B. (1994). *Two-Person Bargaining Experiments with Incomplete Information.* Berlin: Springer-Verlag.

Lancaster, C. (1990). *ADR Round Table.* Fort Belvoir, VA: U.S. Army Corps of Engineers.

Le Poole, S. (1991). *Never Take No For an Answer.* London: Kegan Paul.

Lewicki, R. and Litterer, J. (1985). *Negotiation.* Homewood, IL: Richard D. Irwin.

Lewicki R. and Bazerman, M. (1986). *Research in Negotiations.* Greenwich CT: JAI Press.

Linhart, P. *et. al.* (1992). *Bargaining with Incomplete Information.* San Diego: Academic Press.

Lyou, J. (1990). *The Social Psychology of U.S.-Soviet Arms Control Negotiations: the Role and Experience of the U.S. Negotiator and Delegation.* Unpublished doctoral dissertation.

Maslow, A. (1954). *Motivation and Personality,* New York: Harper and Row.

Mnookin, R. (1993). *Why Negotiations Fail.* Stanford, CA: Stanford Center on Conflict and Negotiation, Stanford University.

Morrison, W. (1994). *The Human Side of Negotiations.* Malabar, FL: Krieger.

Murnighan, J. (1991). *The Dynamics of Bargaining Games.* Englewood Cliffs, NJ: Prentice Hall.

Murnighan, J. (1992). *Bargaining Games: a New Approach to Strategic Thinking in Negotiations*. New York: W. Morrow.

Nagel, S. and Mills, M. (1990). *Multi-Criteria Methods for Alternative Dispute Resolution with Microcomputer Software Applications*. New York: Quorum Books.

Neale, M. and Bazerman, M. (1991). *Cognition and Rationality in Negotiation*. New York: Maxwell Macmillan International.

Neale, M. and Bazerman M. (1991). *Negotiator Cognition and Rationality*. New York: Free Press.

Newsom, D. (1992). *Can Negotiation be Taught?*. Washington, DC: Institute for the Study of Diplomacy, Georgetown University.

Nierenberg, G. (1991). *The Complete Negotiator*. New York: Berkley Books.

Nierenberg, J. and Ross, I. (1985). *Women and the Art of Negotiating*. New York: Simon and Schuster.

Peters, H. (1992). *Axiomatic Bargaining Game Theory*. Boston: Kluwer Academic Publishers.

Pollan, S. (1994). *The Total Negotiator*. New York: Avon Books.

Pritzker, D. and Dalton, D. (1990). *Negotiated Rulemaking Sourcebook*. Washington, DC: Office of the Chairman, Administrative Conference of the U.S.

Pruitt, D, (1988). *Negotiation Behavior*. New York: Academic Press

Pruitt, D. and Carnevale, P. (1993). *Negotiation in Social Conflict*. Pacific Grove, CA: Brooks/Cole Pub. Co.

Putnam, L., and Roloff, M. (1992). *Communication and Negotiation*. Newbury Park, CA: Sage.

Rabin, M. (1991). *Reneging and Renegotiation*. Berkeley, CA: University of California.

Rahim, M. (1990). *Theory and Research in Conflict Management*. Westport, CT: Greenwood Publishing Group.

Rahim, M. (1989). *Managing Conflict: An Interdisciplinary Approach*. New York: Praeger.

Raiffa, H. (1982). *Art and Science of Negotiation*. Cambridge, MA: Harvard University Press.

Ramundo, B. (1992). *Effective Negotiation*. Cambridge: Oelgeshalger, Gunn and Hain.

Rojot, J. (1991). *Negotiation: from Theory to Practice*. Houndmills, Basingstoke, UK: Macmillan.

Ross, L. (1993). *Reactive Devaluation in Negotiation and Conflict Resolution*. Stanford, CA: Stanford Center on Conflict and Negotiation, Stanford University.

Roth A. (1985). *Game-Theoretic Models of Bargaining*. Cambridge: Cambridge University Press.

Rubin, J. and Brown, B. (1975). *The Social Psychology of Bargaining and Negotiation*. New York: Academic Press.

Rubin, J. Pruitt, D. and Kim, S. (1994) *Social Conflict: Escalation, Stalemate, and Settlement* (2nd ed). New York: McGraw-Hill.

Rusk, T. (1993). *The Power of Ethical Persuasion: from Conflict to Partnership at Work and in Private Life*. New York, NY: Viking.

Saaty, T. and Alexander, J. (1989). *Conflict Resolution*. Westport, CT: Greenwood Publishing Group.

Sager, T. (1994). *Communicative Planning Theory*. Brookfield: Avebury.

Sandole, D. (1987). *Conflict Management and Problem Solving: Interpersonal to International Applications*. New York: New York University Press.

Sandole, D. and Merwe, H. (1993). *Conflict Resolution Theory and Practice: Integration and Application*. New York: St. Martin's Press.

Schoenfield, M. and Schoenfield, R. (1991). *The McGraw-Hill 36-Hour Negotiating Course*. New York: McGraw-Hill.

Schoonmaker, A. (1989). *Negotiate to Win: Gaining the Psychological Edge*. Englewood Cliffs, NJ: Prentice Hall.

Shafir, E. (1992). *Thinking through Uncertainty*. Stanford, CA: Stanford Center on Conflict and Negotiation, Stanford University,.

Shenk, M. (1993). *The Virtue of Generosity and the Flexible Prisoner's Dilemma Computer Model*. Stanford, CA: Stanford Center on Conflict and Negotiation, Stanford University.

Shubik, M. (1982). *Game Theory in the Social Sciences*. Cambridge: MIT Press.

Singer, L. (1990). *Settling Disputes*. Boulder, CO: Westview.

Skopec, E. (1994). *Everthing's Negotiable--When You Know How to Play the Game*. New York: American Management Association.

Sochynsky, Y. (1992). *California ADR Practice Guide*. Colorado Springs, CO: Shepard's/McGraw-Hill.

Sparks, D. (1993). *The Dynamics of Effective Negotiation*. Houston: Gulf Pub. Co.

Stark, P. (1994). *It's Negotiable: The How-to Handbook of Win/Win Tactics*. San Diego: Pfeiffer.

Steele, P. *et. al*. (1989). *It's a Deal: A Practical Negotiation Handbook*. New York: McGraw-Hill.

Thomson, W., and Lensberg, T. (1989). *Axiomatic Theory of Bargaining with a Variable Number of Agents*. New York: Cambridge University Press.

Tirella, O. and Bates, G. (1993). *Win-Win Negotiating: A Professional's Playbook*. New York, NY: American Society of Civil Engineers.

Tversky, A. (1992). *Choice under Conflict*. Stanford, CA: Stanford Center on Conflict and Negotiation, Stanford University.

Tversky, A. (1992). *The Disjunction Effect in Choice under Uncertainty*. Stanford, CA: Stanford Center on Conflict and Negotiation, Stanford University.

Ueki, Y. (1989). *Politics of Issue Linkage and Delinkage: An Analysis of Japanese-Soviet Negotiations*. Unpublished doctoral dissertation.

Uhlich, G. (1990). *Descriptive Theories of Bargaining: an Experimental Analysis of Two- and Three-Person Characteristic Function Bargaining*. New York: Springer.

Ury, W., *et. al*. (1988). *Getting Disputes Resolved*. San Francisco: Jossey-Bass.

Ury, W. (1993). *Getting Past No: Negotiating Your Way from Confrontation to Cooperation*. New York: Bantam.

Van Opstal, D. (1989). *View from the Decision Makers*. Washington, DC: Center for Strategic and International Studies.

Varoufakis, Y. (1991). *Rational Conflict*. Oxford, UK: Blackwell.

Von Neumann, J. and Morgenstern, O. (1944). *Theory of Games and Economic Behavior*. New York: John Wiley.

Wall, J. (1989). *Negotiation: Theory and Practice*. Glenview, IL: Scott Foresman

Walton, R. (1987). *Managing Conflict*. Reading, MA: Addison-Wesley Publishing

Warham, S. (1993). *Primary Teaching and the Negotiation of Power*. London: Paul Chapman Publishing.

Warne, T. (1994). *Partnering for Success*. New York, NY: ASCE Press.

Wheeler, M. (1990). *Promoting Negotiation: Yes in my Backyard?*. Cambridge, MA: Center for Real Estate Development, Massachusetts Institute of Technology.

Wilson, R. (1993). *Strategic and Informational Barriers to Negotiation*. Stanford, CA: Stanford Center on Conflict and Negotiation, Stanford University.

Woolf, B. (1990). *Friendly Persuasion: My Life as a Negotiator*. New York: Putnam.

Young, H. (1991). *Negotiation Analysis*. Ann Arbor: University of Michigan Press.

Young, O. (1975). *Bargaining: Formal Theories of Negotiation*. Urbana: University of Illinois.

International Conflict

Acheson, D. (1958). *Meetings at the Summit: a Study in Diplomatic Method*. Durham, NH: University of New Hampshire.

Anstey, M. (1991). *Negotiating Conflict: Insights and Skills for Negotiators and Peacemakers*. Kenwyn, South Africa: Juta and Co.

Antokol, N. and Nudell, M. (1990). *No One a Neutral: Political Hostage-Taking in the Modern World.* Medina, OH: Alpha Publications.

Barker, R. (1980). *Not Here, But in Another Place.* New York: St. Martin's.

Benjamin, M. (1990). *Splitting the Difference: Compromise and Integrity in Ethics and Politics.* Lawrence, Kansas: University Press of Kansas.

Bennett, P. (1989). *The Soviet Union and Arms Control: Negotiation Strategy and Tactics.* New York: Praeger

Bercovitch, J., and Rubin, J. (1992). *Mediation in International Relations: Multiple Approaches to Conflict Management.* New York: St. Martin's Press.

Berridge, G. (1994). Talking to the Enemy: *How States without Diplomatic Relations Communicate.* New York: St. Martin's Press.

Bialer, S. and Mandelbaum, M. (1988). *Gorbachev's Russia and American Foreign Policy.* Boulder, CO: Westview.

Blair, D. (1993). *Trade Negotiations in the OECD: Structures, Institutions, and States.* London: Routledge, Chapman and Hall.

Blaker, M. (1977). *Japanese International Negotiation.* New York: Columbia University.

Bolz, F. and Hershey, E. (1979). *Hostage Cop.* New York: Rawson, Wade Publishers.

Brady, L. (1991). *The Politics of Negotiation: America's Dealings with Allies, Adversaries, and Friends.* Chapel Hill: University of North Carolina Press.

Brannen, C., and Wilen, T. (1993). *Doing Business with Japanese Men: a Woman's Handbook.* Berkeley, CA: Stone Bridge Press.

Brzoska, M., and Pearson, F. (1994). *Arms and Warfare: Escalation, De-escalation, and Negotiation.* Columbia, SC: University of South Carolina Press.

Callieres F. de (1716 reissued 1976). *On the Manner of Negotiating with Princes.* Notre Dame, IN: Notre Dame University Press.

Carter, J. (1984). *Negotiation: The Alternative to Hostility.* Mercer University Press.

Child, J. (1992). *The Central American Peace Process, 1983-1991: Sheathing Swords, Building Confidence.* Boulder: L. Rienner Publishers.

Christopher, W. (1985). *American Hostages in Iran.* New Haven: Yale University Press.

Chu, C. (1991). *The Asian Mind Game: Unlocking The Hidden Agenda of the Asian Business Culture--A Westerner's Survival Manual.* New York: Rawson Associates.

Cohen, R. (1987). *The Art of Diplomatic Signalling.* White Plains, NY: Longmans.

Cohen, R. (1991). *Negotiating Across Cultures: Communication Obstacles in International Diplomacy.* Washington, DC: United States Institute of Peace.

Davis, J., *et. al.* (1992). *Analytic Support for Peace Talks.* Langley, VA: Center for the Study of Intelligence.

Downs, G. and Rocke, D. (1990). *Tacit Bargaining, Arms Races, and Arms Control.* Ann Arbor: University of Michigan Press.

Eban, A. (1983). *The New Diplomacy.* New York: Random House.

English, L. (1995). *Business Across Cultures.* Reading, MA: Addison-Wesley Pub. Co.

Fisher, R. (1978). *International Mediation: A Working Guide.* New York: International Peace Academy.

Fisher. R. (1990). *Social Psychology of Intergroup and International Conflict Resolution.* New York: Springer-Verlag.

Foster, D. (1992). *Bargaining Across Borders: How to Negotiate Business Successfully Anywhere in the World.* New York: McGraw-Hill.

Garfinkle, A. (1991). *The Devil and Uncle Sam: A User's Guide to the Friendly Tyrants Dilemma.*

Gercik, P. (1992). *On Track with the Japanese: A Case-by-Case Approach to Building Successful Relationships.* New York: Kodansha International.

Gerson, A. (1991). *The Kirkpatrick Mission: Diplomacy Without Apology.* New York: The Free Press.

Goodman, A. and Clemens, S. (1992). *Making Peace: the United States and Conflict Resolution.* Boulder, CO: Westview Press.

Graham, J. and Sano, Y. (1989). *Smart Bargaining: Doing Business with the Japanese.* New York: Harper and Row, Ballinger Division.

Griffin, T. *et. al.* (1990). *The Global Negotiator.* New York: Harper.

Gulliver, P. (1979). *Disputes and Negotiations: A Cross-Cultural Perspective.* New York: Academic Press.

Hendon, D. and Hendon R. (1990). *World-class Negotiating: Dealmaking in the Global Marketplace.* New York: John Wiley and Sons, Inc.

Hume, C. (1991). *Negotiations Before Peacekeeping.* New York, NY: International Peace Academy.

Ikle, F. (1964). *How Nations Negotiate.* Millwood, NY: Krauss.

Ikle, F. (1971). *Every War Must End.* New York: Columbia University.

Jonsson, C. (1990). *Communication in International Bargaining.* London: Pinter.

Joy, C. (1970). *How Communists Negotiate.* Santa Monica, CA: Fidelis Publishers, Inc.

Kaufmann, J. (1989). *Effective Negotiation: Case Studies in Conference Diplomacy.* Norwell, MA: Kluwer Academic Publishers.

Kenna, P. and Lacy, S. (1994). *Business France: a Practical Guide to Understanding French Business Culture.* Lincolnwood, IL: NTC Business Books.

Kenna, P. and Lacy, S. (1994). *Business Germany: a Practical Guide to Understanding German Business Culture.* Lincolnwood, IL: NTC Business Books.

Kenna, P. and Lacy, S. (1994). *Business Japan: a Practical Guide to Understanding Japanese Business Culture.* Lincolnwood, IL: NTC Business Books.

Kenna, P. and Lacy, S. (1994). *Business Mexico: a Practical Guide to Understanding Mexican Business Culture.* Lincolnwood, IL: NTC Business Books.

King, J. (1994). *Handshake in Washington: the Beginning of Middle East Peace.* Reading: Ithaca Press.

Kinney, D. (1989). *National Interest, National Honor: the Diplomacy of the Falklands Crisis.* New York: Praeger.

Kissinger, H. (1979). *White House Years.* Boston: Little, Brown and Company.

Kissinger, H. (1982). *Years of Turmoil.* Boston, Little, Brown and Company.

Kissinger, H. (1994). *Diplomacy.* New York: Simon and Schuster.

Kissinger, H. (n.d). *A World Restored: Castlereagh, Metternich and the Restoration of Peace 1812-1822.* Boston: Hougton Mifflin.

Korzenny, F. *et. al.* (1990). *Communicating for Peace: Diplomacy and Negotiation.* Newbury Park, CA: Sage.

Kremenyuk, V. (1991). *International Negotiation: Analysis, Issues.* San Francisco: Jossey-Bass.

Kriesberg, L., and Thorson, S. (1991). *Timing the De-Escalation of International Conflicts.* Syracuse, NY: Syracuse University Press.

Kriesberg, L. *et. al.* (1989). *Intractable Conflicts and Their Transformation.* Syracuse NY: Syracuse University Press.

Kriesberg, L. (1992). *International Conflict Resolution: The US-USSR and Middle East Cases.* New Haven, CT: Yale University Press.

Kull, S. (1988). *Minds at War: Nuclear Reality and the Inner Conflicts of Defense Policy.* New York: Basic Books.

Kupperman, R. and Mazarr, M. (1991). *Improving International Crisis Communications: The Final Report of the CSIS Study Group on International Crisis Communication.* Washington, DC: Center for Strategic and International Studies.

Lakos, A. (1989). *International Negotiations: A Bibliography.* Boulder: Westview Press.

Lanier, A. (1992). *The Rising Sun on Main Street: Working with the Japanese*. Yardley-Morrisville, AU:: International Information Associates.

Lebow, R. (1987). *Nuclear Crisis Management: A Dangerous Illusion*. Ithaca, NY: Cornell.

Lynn-Jones, S. *et. al* (1990). *Nuclear Diplomacy and Crisis Management: An International Security Reader*. Cambridge, MA.: MIT Press.

Mautner-Markhof, F. (1989). *Processes of International Negotiations*. Boulder: Westview Press.

McCall, J. and Warrington, M. (1989). *Marketing by Agreement: A Cross-Cultural Approach to Business Negotiations*. New York: Wiley.

Mee, C. (1980). *The End of Order*. New York: Dutton.

Milner, H. (1988). *Resisting Protectionism: Global Industries and the Politics of International Trade*. Princeton, NJ: Princeton University.

Moran, R. and Stripp, W. (1991). *Dynamics of Successful International Business Negotiations*. Houston: Gulf Publishing.

Moreno, D. (1994). *The Struggle for Peace in Central America*. Gainesville: University Press of Florida.

Morgan, T. Clifton (1994). *Untying the Knot of Fear: A Bargaining Theory of International Crises*. Ann Arbor: University of Michigan Press.

Nicholson H. (1964). *Diplomacy*. New York: Oxford.

Noble, G. (1992). *Flying Apart? Japanese-American Negotiations Over the FSX Fighter Plane*. Berkeley: International and Area Studies, University of California, Berkeley.

Perry, M. (1994). *A Fire in Zion: the Israeli-Palestinian Search for Peace*. New York: Morrow.

Pye, L. (1992). *Chinese Negotiating Style: Commercial Approaches and Cultural Principles*. New York: Quorum Books.

Rasmussen, J. *et. al.* (1992). *Conflict Resolution in the Middle East: Simulating a Diplomatic Negotiation Between Israel and Syria*. Washington, DC: United States Institute of Peace Press.

Rossman, M. (1990). *The International Businesswoman of the 1990s: a Guide to Success in the Global Marketplace*. New York: Praeger.

Rowland, D. (1993). *Japanese Business Etiquette: A Practical Guide to Success with the Japanese*. New York: Warner Books.

Rummel, R. (n.d.). *Understanding Conflict and War*. New York: Norton.

Salacuse, J. (1991). *Making Global Deals: What Every Executive Should Know about Negotiating Abroad*. New York: Times Books.

Silkenat, J. and Aresty, J. (1994). *The ABA Guide to International Business Negotiations: a Comparison of Cross-Cultural Issues and Successful Approaches*. Chicago, IL: American Bar Association.

Smith, D. and Wells, L. (1975). *Negotiating Third World Mineral Agreements*. Cambridge, MA: Ballinger

Smith, R. (1989). *Negotiating with the Soviets*. New York: Midland.

Smoke, R. (1987). *Paths to Peace: Exploring the Feasibility of Sustainable Peace*. Boudler, CO: Westview.

Solomon, R. (1994). *Chinese Political Negotiating Behavior: An Interpretive Assessment*. Santa Monica, CA: Rand.

Stein, J. (1989). *Getting to the Table: the Processes of International Prenegotiation*. Baltimore: Johns Hopkins University Press.

Sunshine, R. (1990). *Negotiating for International Development: a Practitioner's Handbook*. Norwell, MA: Kluwer Academic Publishers.

Tacsan, J. (1992). *The Dynamics of International Law in Conflict Resolution*. Dordrecht: M. Nijhoff.

Telhami, S. (1990). *Power and Leadership in International Bargaining: the Path to the Camp David Accords*. New York: Columbia University Press.

Thompson, K. (1991). *Negotiating Arms Control: Missed Opportunities and Limited Successes*. Lanham, Md.: Miller Center, University of Virginia.

Webster-Doyle, T. (1990). *Tug of War: Peace through Understanding Conflict*. Middlebury, VT: Atrium Society

Whelan, J. (1983). *Soviet Diplomacy and Negotiating Behavior.* Boulder, CO: Westview Press.

Wilhelm, A. (1991). *The Chinese at the Negotiating Table: Style and Characteristics.* Washington, DC: National Defense University Press.

Williams, A. (1992). *Many Voices: Multilateral Negotiations in the World Arena.* Boulder, CO: Westview Press.

Zartman, I. William (1994). *International Multilateral Negotiation: Approaches to the Management of Complexity.* San Francisco: Jossey-Bass.

Organizational Conflict

Aggens, L. (1991). *When People Complain: Using Communication, Negotiation and Problem Solving to Resolve Complaints.* Ft. Belvoir, VA: US Army Corps of Engineers.

Albrecht, K., and Albrecht, S. (1993). *Added Value Negotiating: the Breakthrough Method for Building Balanced Deals.* Homewood, IL: Business One Irwin.

American Arbitration Association (1991). *The Arbitration of Construction Disputes: A Selected Bibiliography of Literature Published From 1980-1990.* New York: Author.

Bacharach, S. and Lawler E. (1980). *Power and Politics in Organizations: The Social Psychology of Conflict, Coalitions, and Bargaining.* San Francisco: Jossey-Bass.

Barlow, C. and Eisen, G. (1983). *Purchasing Negotiations.* Boston: CBI Publishing.

Bastress, R. and Harbaugh, J. (1990). *Interviewing, Counseling, and Negotiating: Skills for Effective Representation.* Boston: Little, Brown.

Bazerman M. *et. al.* (1991). *Research on Negotiation in Organizations.* Greenwich, CT: JAI.

Bergman, T. and Vokema, R. (1989). *Managing Conflict: An Interdisciplinary Approach.* New York: Praeger.

Blanchard, O. (1991). *Wage Bargaining And Unemployment Persistence.* Cambridge, MA: National Bureau of Economic Research.

Brand, N. (1987). *Labor Arbitration: The Strategy of Persuasion.* New York: Practising Law Institute.

Brown, L. (1983). *Managing Conflict at Organizational Interfaces.* Reading, MA: Addison-Wesley.

Carlisle, J. and Parker, R. (1989). *Beyond Negotiation: Redeeming Customer-Supplier Relationships.* New York: Wiley.

Coulson, R. (1981). *The Termination Handbook.* New York: Free Press.

Curtis, R. (1983). *How to Be Your Own Literary Agent.* Boston: Houghton Mifflin.

Doyle, M. and Strauss, D. (1986). *How to Make Meetings Work.* New York: Jove.

Elkouri, F. and Elkouri, E. (1985). *How Arbitration Works.* 4th ed. Washington, DC: BNA Books.

Freund, J. (1975). *Anatomy of a Merger: Strategies and Techniques for Negotiating Corporate Acquisitions.* New York: Law Journal Seminars Press.

Hill, M. and Sinicropi, A. (1987). *Evidence in Arbitration.* 2d ed. Washington, DC: BNA Books.

Hoffman, T. (1984). *How to Negotiate Successfully in Real Estate.* New York: Simon and Schuster.

Hogg, M. and Abrams, D. (1988). *Social Identification: A Social Psychology of Intergroup Relations and Group Processes.* London: Routlege.

Holmes, G., and Glaser, S. (1991). *Business-to-Business Negotiation.* Boston: Butterworth-Heinemann.

Hopkins, T. (1982). *How to Master the Art of Selling.* New York: Warner.

International Industrial Relations Association (1989). *Current Issues in Labour Relations: An International Perspective.* Hamburg: Author.

Jackson, M. (1988). *Selling: The Personal Force in Marketing.* John Wiley and Sons.

Kennedy, G. (1994). *Field Guide to Negotiation: a Glossary of Essential Tools and Concepts for Today's Manager.* Boston, MA: Harvard Business School Press.

Kennedy, G. *et. al.* (1982). *Managing Negotiations.* Englewood Cliffs, NJ: Prentice Hall.

Kennedy, M. (1982). *Salary Strategies.* New York: Ransom, Wade Publishers, Inc.

Lax, D. and Sebenius, J. (1986). *The Manager as Negotiator.* New York: Free Press.

Loughram, C. (1984). *Negotiating a Labor Contract: A Management Handbook.* Washington, DC: BNA Books.

McCall, J. and Warrington, M. (1984). *Marketing By Agreement: A Cross-Cultural Approach to Business Negotiations.* John Wiley and Sons.

McVay, B. (1987). *Getting Started in Federal Contracting.* Woodbridge, VA: Panoptic Enterprises.

Miller, P and Bregman, D. (1987). *The Common-Sense Guide to Successful Real Estate Negotiation.* New York: Harper and Row.

Morrison, W. (1985). *Prenegotiation Planning Book.* New York: John Wiley and Sons.

Nudell, M. and Antokol, N. (1988). *The Handbook for Effective Emergency and Crisis Management.* Lexington, MA: Lexington Books.

Osborne, M. and Rubinstein, A. (1990). *Bargaining and Markets.* San Diego: Academic Press.

Paterson, L. (1990). *Negotiating Employee Resignations.* Carlsbad, CA: Parker and Son Publications.

Percelay, B. and Arnold, P. (1986). *Packaging Your Home for Profit.* New York: Little, Brown.

Peters, E. (1955). *Strategy and Tactics in Labor Negotiations.* New London, CT: National Foremen's Institute.

Pickerell, J. (1989). *Negotiating Stock Photo Prices.* Rockville, MD: Pickerell Marketing.

Potapchuk, W. *et. al.* (1990). *Getting to the Table: a Guide for Senior Managers, Alternative Dispute Resolutions* [sic]. Fort Belvoir, VA: U.S. Army Corps of Engineers.

Putnam, L. and Roloff, M. eds. (1991). *Communication Perspectives on Negotiation.* Newbury Park, CA: Sage.

Ramundo, B. (1994). *The Bargaining Manager: Enhancing Organizational Results through Effective Negotiation.* Westport, Conn.: Quorum Books.

Rubin, P. (1990). *Managing Business Transactions: Controlling the Cost of Coordinating, Communicating, and Decision Making.* New York: Maxwell Macmillan International.

Sharp, W. (1993). *Collective Bargaining in the Public Schools.* Madison, WI: Brown and Benchmark.

Sheppard, B. *et. al.* (1990). *Research on Negotiation in Organizations.* Greenwich, CT: JAI

Staudohar, P. (1986). *The Sports Industry and Collective Bargaining.* Ithaca: Cornell.

Stulberk, J. (1987). *Taking Charge: Managing Conflict.* Lexington, MA: Lexington Books.

Tarrant, J. (1976). *How to Negotiate a Raise.* New York: Van Nostrand-Reinhold

Tarrant, J. (1985). *Perks and Parachutes: Negotiating Your Executive Employment Contract.* New York: Simon and Schuster.

Torrington, D. (1991). *Management Face-to-Face.* New York: Prentice Hall.

Westin, A. and Feliu, A. (1988). *Resolving Employment Disputes Without Litigation.* Washington, DC: BNA Books.

Yeschke, C. (1987). *Interviewing: An Introduction to Interrogation.* Springfield, IL: Charles C. Thomas.

Journals

American Bar Foundation Research Journal
Annual of Power and Conflict
Annual Review of Conflict Knowledge and Conflict Resolution
Bulletin of Peace Proposals
Bulletin of Peace Research
Choice
Conflict
Conflict Management and Peace Science
Conflict Quarterly
Conflict Resolution
Cooperation and Conflict
Foreign Affairs Quarterly
International Journal of Conflict Resolution
International Journal of Group Tensions
Journal of Conflict Resolution
Journal of Dispute Resolution
Journal of International Business Studies
Journal of Organizational Behavior
Journal of Peace Science
Journal of Policy Analysis and Management
Mediation Quarterly
Negotiation Quarterly
Resolve
Studies in Conflict and Terrorism
Terrorism
Theory and Research in Conflict Management

About the Author and Bibliographers

David Churchman is chairman of the Behavioral Science Graduate Program and coordinator of the MA program in Negotiation and Conflict Management at California State University Dominguez Hills. He also is co-founder and treasurer of Wildlife on Wheels, which provides live-animal environmental education programs to schools in the Los Angeles area. His avocations include chess, cooking, rifle marksmanship, photography, and travel.

Kelly Kartchner, who prepared the bibliography, and Randy Hatago who updated it, are graduate students in the MA program in Negotiation and Conflict Management at California State University Dominguez Hills. Ms. Kartchner is the coordinator for group purchasing services at Purchase Connection, a national group purchasing organization in the health care industry. Mr. Hatago is a student assistant in the research department of the university library.